THE SPIRIT
OF THE
EARTH

THE SPIRIT OF THE EARTH

A
Teilhard
Centennial Celebration

Edited by
Jerome Perlinski

The Seabury Press / New York

1981
The Seabury Press
815 Second Avenue
New York, N.Y. 10017

Printed in the United States of America

Library of Congress Cataloging in Publication Data

Main entry under title:

The Spirit of the earth.

1. Teilhard de Chardin, Pierre—Addresses, essays,
lectures.   I. Perlinski, Jerome.
B2430.T374S76   194   80-28380
ISBN 0-8164-2298-2

CONTENTS

Introduction 1
Jerome Perlinski

PART ONE BODY / MIND

CULTURAL APPRENTICESHIP 17
William R. Coulson

CHANGING VIEWS OF CREATIVITY AND
EVOLUTION 33
Willis W. Harman

LITERACY, EVOLUTION, AND
DEVELOPMENT 49
Robert A. Rubinstein and Sol Tax

PART TWO MIND / SPIRIT

THE VISION IS THE REALITY 67
Elise Boulding

LOVE'S CONSPIRATORS:
BUILDERS OF EARTH-HOUSE-HOLD 85
Francis Tiso

PART THREE SPIRIT / SOCIETY

TOWARD AN EVOLUTIONARY THEOLOGY 105
Kenneth E. Boulding

MY FIVE TEILHARDIAN ENLIGHTENMENTS 117
Robert Muller

MYRIAD SPECKS / TEASING GRACE 131
Paolo Soleri

Contributors 145

INTRODUCTION

Jerome Perlinski

I

I am, like you, another one of them, a child of violence. With my parents before me and theirs before them, I have never really known a time of social tranquility and peace.

When my great-grandfather, a village mayor near Warsaw, urged his son Andrew to escape impressment into the Russian Army, he undoubtedly said, "Go to America; otherwise they'll send you to Siberia to fight the Japanese." So Andrew "stayed out" of the Russo-Japanese War of 1905. He came instead to the land of promise where he raised corn and pigs, cabbages and chickens on a farm in Indiana.

But once again he was forced to move, this time to Chicago, and again to escape military conscription. "They'll send me to Germany to fight the Kaiser," he probably said in 1917. And he became a factory worker (these were exempted from the draft since they supplied needed war matériel) and again "stayed out" of a war. (A year or two later news reached him that his father, the old *bürgermeister*, had been shot on the steps of the village church, protecting it against the advancing Bolsheviks.)

I was already born when *my* father's factory converted to "war work" in World War II. (Did they make bullets, rifles, soldier's canteens?) A damaged finger, its joint lopped off by a punch press, and the factory "war work" helped my father "stay out" of the war. In a four-room Chicago flat, the five of us—mother, father, two sons, a daughter—lived much like the rest of America: on rationed food, trust in Roosevelt, lots of imagination (my father was a springwinder; my earliest toys were mistakes made by the factory "girls"), and the pervasive spirituality of a Polish variant of the Roman Catholic faith.

We burned tapers blessed at Candlemas when fearful thunderheads broke over the city; our throats were blessed, our house was blessed, our flowers, our babies, our sins, our hopes and dreams—all made holy. My family for generations were not only loyal, but generous, serfs of the Church. There is a long history of priests and nuns, and other relatives occupying mostly humble positions: bell ringers and priests' servants, church secretaries, janitors, founders of societies, workers at carnivals, bingoes, and picnics.

For me the Church represented culture, meaning, beauty, the future in an otherwise bleak, gray, and violent world. I continued the family tradition and joined, at seventeen years old, a religious order where in long years of medievally disciplined life I was made privy to the secrets of the Church's power.

At nineteen I read Teilhard de Chardin's *The Phenomenon of Man.* I read it all at once, breathing hard and feeling the ecstasy of freedom, in a basement student lounge in St. Louis. Or rather, the ecstasy of knowing with my whole being that I had always been right, for the book was an affirmation, really, of one's whole life, of one's direction, of *my* direction.

(In the more than twenty years that I have been talking and writing about Teilhard—indeed much of my professional life has been spent specifically in this work—the reaction of those many who have "caught fire" by reading him, has been much the same: a sense of joy, of at last not being alone, a tremendous "yes." Or as Teilhard himself put it, of finding a "way out" from under the lowering clouds of an exhausted culture.)

But as a child of violence, I could not accept Teilhard as a "master," a sort of oracle, a cult leader. I had learned my lessons too well. I am, after all, the little blond open-mouthed boy, jumping about and shouting, "Unconditional surrender, Yeaaa!"; I am a serious, already alienated four-eyed schoolboy waking up on cold Chicago mornings to "Porkchop Hill" and Panmunjom; then a struggler in a changeless, airless seminary, crew-cut, "striving for perfection," wrestling with social habits and mindless tradition and the tremendous and terrible ocean of repressed emotion and lack of imagination characteristic of male religious orders, freeing myself from it all in a single jolt, "leaving" religious life as if one were dying, and dying, yes; I am a marcher, black-and-white fasting and keeping vigil in slums and before government buildings; I am a nervous twenty-five-year-old sweating out an A-1 draft status; a striker along with the rest against the cruel bombardment of Cambodia. And I am alive now, like everyone, in the thickening haze of nuclear destruction.

Oh no, after all that I shall not easily sell myself to any teacher. That is the way it must be for me, for us, children of violence. We have learned to trust only our own intuitions, our own experiences. Stripped certainly not of all but of most of the great illusions of happiness and prosperity upon which this epoch, so clearly decisive in humanity's history, is based, we cling only to ourselves, to one another.

We are children of violence, promises unfulfilled, hopes drained, visions clouded, wills enfeebled. The schools, the churches, the overlords in business and government, "superiors" everywhere have told us and told us again and shouted it in our ears: you are a cog in a vast machine, lose yourself in it, your sacrifice is needed, give me your body and your heart and your mind and I will feed it to the merciless and demanding Kali; do not harbor personal dreams; do not dress in "crazy" clothes; do what is useful and profitable; keep yourself busy, achieve, strive, struggle, make yourself comfortable, lose yourself in anything but in yourself.

They dinned it in our ears until we believed them. We do believe them; we find ourselves saying the same things to our children in our own various ways. For many of us this message of restraining frustration and promised doom, of habitual, conventional, middle-class imitations of life has become *our* way, *my* way, a tremendous "no" to all that is free, vibrant, and receptive.

We have been pressed to the limit. We understand completely and intuitively what Teilhard means when he writes, "The first thing I saw was that only man can be of any use to man in finding the secret of the world."

From each other, from our lives, miserable or honorable as they may be, from our individual stories, from brief pulses of intuition and flashes of beauty, we have fashioned another message that is, almost miraculously, being heard even beyond the conformity and suffusing hopelessness. This message quickens my life and that of others to such an extent that to our title, "children of violence," we feel confident to add, "children of light."

How was it for you? What is your story? How did you manage to recognize that the darkness is only a part of existence? Through the conquest of fear or pain? A great book? Teilhard? Work? Loneliness? The Grand Canyon? How did you discover *yin* and *yang*?

For me freedom has always seemed to be everywhere, making me always certain that the fog of violence is but a fog, obscuring the dazzling diaphany of life as it could be. The same blond boy who thundered vengeance on the Japanese, and who reeled in horror at the sight of Hitler's mangled victims, this same blond boy lay on his stomach in a patch of grass, a speck among the million backyards of industrial Chicago, and believed, *believed* in the greatness and desirability of goodness, truth, and beauty.

Through the bit of personalism of Emmanuel Suhard and the *Jocist* movement which seeped through the pedestrian haze of the 1950s, I learned to "observe, judge, and act" about necking and petting and lying, but also about racial prejudice and injustice. I brought black people home to meet my apprehensive parents; later in St. Louis I *believed* that my work in its slums would hasten freedom for all including me; I fought hard against the mechanistic mind-training of the university. To the hilarity of fellow faculty members I renounced academic rank as unworthy of scholars and seekers of the truth; to the dismay of the AAUP, I proposed the abandonment of the tenure system; I helped adolescents distinguish between acid trips and mystical trips and had a few myself.

I felt kin to Whitman, to Nietzsche, to Kazantzakis, Hesse, Maslow, Rogers, and Teilhard. And further back to Kierkegaard, Goethe, Erasmus. And further still even to Jesus and Buddha and Confucius, and the *I Ching,* and the *Baghavad Gita.* And to the great novelists Faulkner, Conrad, Lessing, Steinbeck, Proust, Mann; and to films, and to sex, and to food; to the tiny-acre orchard on which I now dwell; to the immense energy I witnessed in religious and educational reform; in the women's and the gay liberation movements; in the exhilaration and life I find today among the Teilhard Foundation network.

That is how it was for me. Against the gigantic, apocalyptic backdrop of our dying culture, these instances of conscious living convince me that I am a child of light as well as a child of violence.

Think for a moment how it was for you. It is a question of worth and value, of *personal* worth and *personal* value; a conviction that no matter how you are pounded and pummeled into being a consumer, a citizen, a father, a teacher, a worshiper, a student, you spring forth eternally, wholly and completely *you;* a singular, sacred person, center of energy and light, sinking to your knees in obeisance to the laws of heaven and shaking your fist like Zorba, shouting to Olympus, "Am I not a man?" Or with Simone de Beauvoir, believing that "one is not born a woman, one becomes a woman."

All through our lives we have been given this double message: age of gloom and doom, age of human glory; a time of human degradation (ah, we see it daily) and of human deification (in moondust). An age dying, an age being born. A new age, a new time; an old age, a dying time. The Kaliyuga, the Age of Aquarius.

All around the engines of war and greed and despair threaten to drown the countertheme of birth, without which it, violence itself, would lose all meaning.

Have you too felt an affinity for Erasmus's excitement at

being part of a "new age"? Or that of the young Luther? And earlier for Pico, Joachim of Flora, Francis himself; and even back further, for Alexander establishing a new order from the banks of the Indus; or Tut in the daring of his religious transformation; or King Asoka putting down his arms and renouncing war forever?

This book is another beat in the ripening melody I have tried to unfold for you here. The song is ageless, the message the same: Death and Rebirth, the Empty Tomb, the *t'ai chi*, the union of the firmament, the myth of paradise, evolution, a smile, a tear. *There is no other message which can sound even feebly against the deafening cacophony of entropy and death. Only persons, whole, complete persons at one with themselves AND WITH EACH OTHER, are a song pure enough, simple enough to override, once and for all, the noxious harmonies of violence and fate.*

This book then is the celebration of a particular person and of his particular worldview. It is a compilation of personal responses to a singular person: Pierre Teilhard de Chardin.

II

Now his is a fabulous story. Teilhard too was a child of violence and a child of light. His particular search, the "way it was for him," led him from a tired French provincial life to Egypt, China, Burma, Java, South Africa, and finally to the United States.

His was a life of controversy, although at first nothing seemed to indicate this. He came from a family of means in the Auvergne, born a hundred years ago in 1881. His earliest memories tied him strongly to the earth and to the search for something beyond all change:

> As far as I can go back in my childhood, nothing seems to me more characteristic or familiar in my inner disposition than the taste or irresistible need for some "one and only sufficing and necessary" thing: in order to be fully at ease, to be completely happy in the knowledge that "some essential thing" does really exist, to which everything else is no more than an accessory or, maybe,

an embellishment. To know that, and unceasingly to re-
joice in the consciousness of its existence. (The Heart of
Matter," 1950)

The genteel life of the family homes and chateaux continued
in the scholarly and pious surroundings of the Jesuit schools
and seminaries Teilhard attended. Studying in England, he
indulged his passion for geology, met G. B. Dawson and became involved with the Piltdown Man, eventually shown to be a
hoax. Then he taught in Egypt for three years, went on digs,
and drowned himself in the exoticism of the Orient.

This quiet life was shattered in 1914 when he, with several
millions of other European men, was called to the trenches.
The impact of the war, the sheer energy of the war front gave
him an image of a united humanity.

> I think one could show that the front isn't simply the
> firing-line, the exposed area corroded by the conflict of
> nations, but the "front of the wave" carrying the world
> of man toward its new destiny. When you look at it dur-
> ing the night, lit up by flares, after a day of more than
> usual activity, you seem to feel that you're at the final
> boundary between what has already been achieved and
> what is struggling to emerge. (Letter to Claude Ara-
> gonnés, 23 September 1917)

Filled with this new vision, which he felt completely rev-
olutionized our attitude toward the world, he threw himself
into the Paris of the 1920s. He was a vigorous forty-year-old in
1921; witty, handsome, intelligent, mystical—and he was a war
survivor. He wrote experimental essays, gave brilliant lectures,
furthered his career in science and turned his attention to in-
terpreting traditional Christian teachings in the light of evolution and human unity.

Church authorities were aroused and suspicious of this
young priest whose language was that of science rather than
traditional religion, and who seemed to suggest that both were
too narrow for the wide vistas of the contemporary mind. In

the days when religious obedience was still taken for granted, he signed their demands for silence and sailed for China, forbidden thereafter to hold any public position in his native France or to publish or speak out on other than "purely" scientific matters.

In China he established himself as a major force in the scientific community. He worked with Dr. Pei on the Chinese Geological Survey and in the discovery of Peking Man. He made the Yellow Crossing, an expedition across the Gobi sponsored by the Citroën Company. He returned sporadically for short visits to Europe and the United States. He enjoyed the friendship of strong professional women: Lucille Swan, the sculptress; Melvina Hoffman, also a sculptress; the intellectual Jeanne Mortier who later published his works; and the New Yorker Rhoda de Terra.

After World War II Teilhard understood himself to be a world citizen, a "terrestrial." Yet he had no real home. France and Mao's China were now closed to him. He accepted an offer from Paul Fejos of the Wenner-Gren Foundation for Anthropological Research to join him as a Fellow. The last years in America showed that his interests continued in every direction. He showed up at Columbia University; he sat on panels with Margaret Mead, Julian Huxley, Archibald MacLeish, George Gaylord Simpson, Sol Tax; he inspected the early anthropological and paleontological surveys in eastern and southern Africa; he marveled at Broadway's Great White Way and Berkeley's cyclotron, seeing in them both symbols of unified human energy.

Yet because he was forbidden to speak out publicly on his ideas about the central place of the human person, about the growing "noosphere," he was lonely.

One would think that a single ray of this kind of light, falling anywhere on the Noosphere, as a spark, would cause an explosion strong enough to inflame and transform the face of the Earth almost instantaneously. How then can it be that I, looking around me, still intoxicated by what has been shown to me, should find myself alone,

as it were, the only one of my species? The only one to
have *seen?* . . . and so unable, when asked, to cite a single
author, a single text, which might clearly describe the
marvelous "translucence" that has so transfigured everything I see? ("The Christic," March 1955)

Teilhard died on Easter Sunday, 1955, in a Park Avenue
apartment and was buried quietly near Hyde Park, New York.

What is so controversial in this vision of a mild-mannered
scientist? First, evolution. The year in which the Scopes
Monkey Trial in the United States occurred, in which William
Jennings Bryan and Clarence Darrow passionately fought over
the meaning of evolution and its consequences, Teilhard received his exile orders over the very same issue. In his mind,
there was no doubt about evolution. A key to understanding
evolution was the human:

> It is an extraordinary thing. For a century scientists have
> been examining with unheard-of subtlety and daring
> the mysteries of the atoms of matter and of the living
> cell. They have weighed the electron and the stars. They
> have divided the plant and animal world into hundreds
> of thousands of species . . . they are trying to analyze the
> driving forces in human psychology or to bring out the
> laws that govern the exchange of products and services
> in the increasing complexity of society. And yet, with all
> this work going on, hardly anyone has yet thought of
> asking the question that really matters: What precisely is
> the phenomenon of man? In other words and more
> exactly, what place is held, and what purpose is fulfilled,
> in the observed development of the world, by the as-
> tonishing power of thought? ("The Phenomenon of
> Man," November 1930)

And what is the secret of the future?

> With the support of what religion and science have been
> teaching me for the last fifty years, I have tried in this to
> make my way out into the open. I wanted to get clear of
> the fog and see things as they really are . . . and the first

thing I saw was that only man can be of any use to man in reading the secret of the world. ("Spirit of the Earth," March 1931)

By following the complex pattern of evolution from subatomic particles to the human brain, Teilhard believed he saw the outlines of the future in the "ultra-human," that massive and incredibly complex organism grown from the common, interdependent, and infinitely various workings of all human minds pointed in a single direction:

No proof exists that Man has come to the end of his potentialities, that he has reached his highest point. On the contrary, everything suggests that at the present time we are entering a peculiarly critical phase of super-humanization. ("Life and Planets," 1946)

The "ultra-human," "planetized" humanity, the "noosphere," "super-life"—these are some of the words with which Teilhard groped to describe the future. He saw the history of the world in the last several hundred years as describing a vast change in human direction. From a common origin, perhaps in eastern or southern Africa, humanity spread around the globe, founding cultures, civilizations, empires, perfecting techniques and ideas. Then five hundred years ago, at the extreme western tip of Portugal, the explorers of the Western World went out, edging around the coasts of Africa, around the Cape of Good Hope, crossing the Atlantic, finally circumnavigating the globe. The rest of this history we know too well: colonialism, development, intense international rivalry, explosive and devastating wars, and an astounding devopment in technology which has brought us so close that almost no one in 1981 is farther distant than the nearest telephone. The species has covered the globe. We find ourselves inextricably intermeshed with one another.

What are the consequences of this view? In politics it means the discovery of new ways of international cooperation and cosmopolitan life, new political systems that enhance human unity and the human person. In economics it encourages cooperation rather than competition. In science and technology it stresses research in new energy sources, in psychic development, in perceiving the earth as a single organism ("Gaia Hypothesis") with a single "spirit of the earth." In religion it demands a transformation of the old local dogmatic spirit to one encompassing all peoples in an open, flexible, and personal dynamic toward an evolving God who is yet to come.

Teilhard's is a powerful and positive voice for a human future, provided that that future is based on the freedom of the whole human person. His is a challenge, not to wreck and destroy the values and institutions of the past, but to build on them to transform them to a planetary, noospheric level.

He believed the time was short for making the decision about a human future. He was concerned about the sources of human energy and how to activate it (the "taste for life"). He understood that the human and free way to bring about planetization is love, which he refused to confound with feelings or ideas, defining it as union with someone toward someone greater:

> Everywhere on earth, at this moment, within the new spiritual atmosphere created by the appearance of the idea of evolution, there float—in a state of extreme mutual sensitivity—the two essential components of the Ultra-human: love of God and faith in the world.

> Everywhere these two components are "in the air": generally, however, they are not strong enough, *both at the same time*, to combine with one another *in one and the same subject.* In me, by pure chance (temperament, education, environment) the proportion of each happens to be favourable, and they fuse together spontaneously. The fusion of the two is still not strong enough to spread explosively, but even so, it is enough to show that such an explosion is possible and that, *sooner or later, the chain reaction will get under way.*

> It is one more proof that if the truth appears once, in one single mind, that is enough to ensure that nothing

can ever prevent it from spreading to everything and
setting it ablaze. ("The Christic," March 1955)

III

The essays in this volume are responses to Teilhard de Chardin's life and to his vision. They are also in their individual
ways their authors' own stories; how it was for them, how they
see the intricate intertwining of dark and light. They speak
about international relations, brain research, personal environment, the themes, the melodies of our own age.

These songs, we hope, will be the beginning of a celebration
for all of us. In mythical ways we seem still to be huddling
around our fires, holding back the fear of the night with our
stories, celebrating our heroes' ways, telling of our own
exploits, our hearts rising in our throats as we hear chanted,
for the thousandth and most necessary of times, the epic of
humanity's struggle to become one.

Robert Müller, Elise Boulding, Willis Harman, William
Coulson, Kenneth Boulding, Paolo Soleri, Francis Tiso, Sol
Tax, and Robert Rubinstein are each a verse in that epic chant.
There are many others.

There is the line about the perfectly ordinary people of sub-
urban Denver who dreamed one evening in Golden, Colorado.
The widespread celebration of the Teilhard centennial in
America, this book, the Teilhard Foundation itself are all results of that dreaming.

There is the bittersweet verse of Mlle. Jeanne Mortier who in
hardship and against all odds published the works of Teilhard
in the stifling atmosphere of the mid 1950s.

And there is that remarkable parenthesis, a lyric tilt only, of
how Seabury's Avery Brooke and I came to do this book.

Millions, billions more verses and couplets still to be added;
millions, billions ever-more-complex rhythms and variations
still to be composed. Until even the immense rambling structures of a Mahabharata or the story of the rise of the West
appear as the tiny, throbbing trills of a single instrument in a
vast universal symphony.

There is, of course, *your* line, *your* couplet, *your* story needing, groaning to be added, to be synthesized into the whole.

The Spirit of the Earth, then, is an invitation to celebration, to enjoy yourself. True, it's a book, and so its activating power must be secondhand and abstract, expressed in words.

As children of violence we've learned and rightly so to mistrust even language, knowing that the word distorts the reality by its own reality. As children of light, however, we know this must be so and accept it. We dare to struggle with the word, against all hope to become.

We will fail. The written word distorts perhaps even more than the spoken word. Only our actions, that is, our free choices, can truly liberate. Even then, deprived of nourishment in imagination and reduced to the shadow of a human, we are even uncertain about the value and meaning of action and whether our dream of liberation is not, like Marley's ghost, just a "bit of mustard."

So our little book of essays can be only an invitation, as I say, to celebrate, to think: how has it been for you, child of violence, child of light?

how are you turning the dark to light?

how are you nurturing flowers in the dung hill?

where are you dreaming dreams?

what fiery trace are you leaving with your passing?

how are you fathering and mothering the infant child born of violence?

how do you complete the unfinished work of your ancestors?

what joyous praise has passed your lips with the urge to kiss and be one?

where in the dim kivas of dying banks and schools and churches, has the smile of recognition and validation and knowing, lit, if just for an instant, the heavy gloom?

how, in plastic kitchens and K-Marts; on jets; in the smooth sure handle of the wheel and the curve of the highway; in the drinking, the smoking, the eating; in MX missiles; in starving children and Cadillacs and Cuisinarts, how have you raised your thin and feeble voice for the dreams of all humanity, for *your* dreams?

how do you, child of violence, child of light, join your anxious, trembling, violent, agonizing, delicious, earthbound, embodied spirit to the growing "spirit of the earth," and thence on "through orbs ascending" to the Oneness that is All and Nothing?

Works Referred to in the Text

Teilhard de Chardin, Pierre. "The Christic." In *The Heart of Matter.* New York: Harcourt Brace Jovanovich, 1978

———. "The Heart of Matter." In *The Heart of Matter.* New York: Harcourt Brace Jovanovich, 1978.

———. "Life and the Planets." In *The Future of Man.* New York: Harper & Row, 1964.

———. "The Spirit of the Earth." In *Human Energy.* New York: Harcourt Brace Jovanovich, 1969.

Part One

BODY/MIND

CULTURAL APPRENTICESHIP

William R. Coulson

Our condition in infancy can be alternatively described as one of egocentricity or of selflessness. In either case, no distinction between self and world is experienced by the infant. Only with further development do we become divided from the world. With this division arise the hazards of belief and their necessity. The occasion of our division from the world marks the birth of our powers of deliberate judgment about reality. It suggests that the course of lifelong development may represent the closing of a circle: we return to a form of merger with the world, this one not inevitable as in childhood, but chosen. This merger can be for good or ill. In its character lie the possibilities of morality, cultural development, and intellectual growth.

The unity with the world that was the infant's birthright has to be earned by adults through the exercise of judgment. The opportunity of the human person is to perceive the good and turn toward it. In addition to our natural appetites in common with lower animals, we have the gift of thought, and with the bestowal of this gift the obligation to use it. I shall argue in this essay that the proper goal of human development is to use our powers of thought to bring ourselves to conform to reality.

That reality itself is in the process of development cannot be denied by one who has studied the work of Pierre Teilhard de Chardin. In *The Future of Man* Teilhard notes:

The existence of an ascendant movement in the Universe has been revealed to us by the study of paleontology. Where is Man to be situated in this line of progress?

The answer is clear. If, as I maintain, the movement of the cosmos towards the highest degree of consciousness is not an optical illusion, but represents the essence of biological evolution, then, in the curve traced by Life, Man is unquestionably situated at the topmost point; and it is he, by his emergence and existence, who finally proves the reality of the trajectory and defines it—"the dot on the i." . . .

Indeed, within the field accessible to our experience, does not the birth of Thought stand out as a critical point through which all the striving of previous ages passes and is consummated—the critical point traversed by consciousness, when, by force of concentration, it ends by reflecting upon itself? (*The Future of Man,* 1964, p. 67)

Culture represents the accumulated self-reflection of humankind. I believe it is imperative today to make a case for cultural apprenticeship, for there is a romantic individualism at large which seems to claim the self-sufficiency of the singular person and which has been encouraged by overgeneralization of the lessons of humanistic therapeutic psychology.

The True Nature of Individuality

The origins of individuality, which culminate in human personhood, can already be traced in life's first emergence 500 million years ago. The precursors of personhood which are represented by the self-controlling shape and structure of the first miniscule specks of living matter were purely vegetative in character. Nonetheless, the bacillus which is our earliest ancestor in the anthropogenetic chain bore the primitive mark of individuality: for the first time in *history* a center of self-interest was established against the background of the *meaninglessness* of inanimate existence. With the origin of life, integrated internal organization had arisen, in which physiological functioning served the purpose of survival. This was an achievement of great moment, followed by others. From this vegetative origin the successive stages of our personhood ascend through *activity, perceptivity,* and finally *responsibility,* each stage representing what Teilhard refers to as steps of increasingly "centered complexity." There can be no question that such is the ascending evolutionary course. Evident in phylogenetic development, it is repeated in every human ontogenesis; just as higher principles have gradually gained control of emerging life forms over the course of evolutionary history, so too can they be seen to have become more prominent and predominant in the human individual's embryonic and infantile development.

We can speak, then, of a kind of personhood which is present even in lower life forms, but it is clear that it reaches its apogee only at the stage of responsibility. Why is this so?

My answer depends on illuminating the contrast between the argument of Michael Polanyi (*Personal Knowledge,* 1958) for the necessity of culture in human development and the recommendation of a group I call "the therapeutic psychologists" (cf., for example, Gordon, *Parent Effectiveness Training,* 1970) that parents withhold the articulation of their values from their children for the sake of their children's psychological growth. The latter is a view developed in psychotherapy and now recommended more widely to enhance the further development of personhood. It sees the articulation of parental values as a barrier to personal development in children and recommends that, as the therapist tries to help a young client find his *own* values, so too must the parent. I believe that if this view becomes normative it will actually *arrest* the further development of the specifically human. As Teilhard has shown us, man's rise from mute beasthood to human personhood has been achieved through the creation of the noosphere. Noogenesis, in the terms of Polanyi's appreciation of Teilhard's discovery, is the "ultimate evolutionary step, by which human knowledge was born. . . . It was achieved by men who, forming societies, invented language and created by it a lasting articulate framework of thought" (*Personal Knowledge,* p. 388). As I take it, the existence of a noosphere specific to the human race means that parents have the responsibility to articulate their ideals for the sake of their children, for "the child achieves responsible personhood by entering a traditional noosphere" (*Personal Knowledge,* pp. 388–89).

The contrary position holds that the preferred role of the parent is as nondirective therapist. The following dialog, recommended in a syndicated psychological advice column, illustrates this role. Mother's therapeutic assignment, in the scene, is to reflect her son's feelings, "not to get involved in his behavior."

> *Michael* (who has just come home after completing his first year of college): I have the greatest girl friend ever.
> *Mother:* Hm.
> *Michael:* I really like her.
> *Mother:* Oh.
> *Michael:* I'm going to see her tomorrow.
> *Mother:* You have a date.
> *Michael:* I met her last week in school when she came to visit Larry, the drummer in our band. She came with us when we played and seemed to enjoy our music. She went with Larry at first, but I could see she liked me. I went to bed with her before I actually liked her. But now I know her and like her a lot.
> *Mother:* (stunned by the outpouring of more information than she cared to hear): Oh, Michael, you met a girl you really like! How exciting!
> *Michael:* She missed the bus back the first night so she stayed over the whole week and I slept with her every night until I had to come home. And now I really like her a lot. I can hardly wait to see her again.
> *Mother:* It sounds like your last week at school was a very happy one.

Michael is satisfied. His good feelings have been reflected back to him. But what about mother? What about her feeling noted by the psychologist, that she is "stunned by the outpouring of more information than she cared to hear"—to say nothing of how her son's reported behavior might clash with her own upbringing and values? In the popular new view of "parenting," mother is to keep her reactions to herself. She is to be but the mirror in which her son dwells on himself. Thus the modern therapeutic household: one person, the teenaged Michael, and two psychological servants, his parents. For the sake of child development, parents are to withhold their world view.

Mutual Responsibility

Realization of the necessity of cultural apprenticeship in carrying forward the thrust of evolution leads to a recommendation in sharp contrast to the psychotherapeutic. This recommendation is that children be drawn further into their parents' world; it is based on the argument that mutual responsibility is a defining characteristic of humankind. It sees cultural growth—and therefore human growth—as imperiled to the extent that generations draw away from one another. It sees psychologism and its recommendation that parents adopt the methods of therapists as promoting that withdrawal. The true parental role, I will hold, is not merely to understand and accept one's children as a therapist would but to guide them in the exploration and expansion of the noosphere, leading the way at first, walking alongside them as they mature, following them as they have children of their own and move into membership in the command generation themselves. There are opportunities for learning which only a parent can provide; there is guidance needed which only inadequately can be offered by a substitute.

Such a view of child-rearing is the only one that I believe a Teilhardian evolutionary perspective supports. "The primeval matrix of life," notes Polanyi in a parallel analysis to Teilhard's, "was inanimate and deathless—subject to neither failure nor suffering" ("Scientific Thought and Social Reality," 1974, p. 128). Only with the rise of life from this matrix was there to be any possibility of individual achievement, or of error; and only with life, of course, death. There is a kind of direct immortality available to unicellular creatures which is not to higher animals. Only with the evolutionary step beyond the protozoa would the greater achievements of augmented self-control become possi-

ble and would personal existence become more obviously finite. The rise of multicellular organisms, Polanyi notes,

> enabled animals to evolve a more complex physiology
> based on sexual reproduction, a manner of propagation
> which greatly strengthened their personhood. The story
> of the Fall presents a strangely apt symbol of this event.
> For as one part of the body took over procreation and
> the animal ceased to survive in its progeny, lust and
> death were jointly invented. And as the achievement of
> metazoic existence established the rudiments of this
> tragic combination, a finite personal destiny arose to
> challenge the surrounding deserts of deathless inani-
> mate matter (*Personal Knowledge,* 1958, pp. 387–88).

Polanyi calls this series of evolutionary achievements "the first
revolution" but also calls it incomplete, "for a self-centered life
ending in death has little meaning." A second revolution would
be necessary, one defined by the creation of a culture as home
for the ideals which we trust to transcend our individual
deaths. This necessity is prefigured in the development of a
nervous system in polycellular organisms and in particular the
formation of organs of sensation.

> The use of sense organs extends the animal's area of
> mental control into the surrounding space. But seeing is
> foreseeing and is hence also believing; perception in-
> volves judgment and the possibility of error. Therefore,
> as the personhood of our ancestors was enriched and
> expanded by the power of new senses, it was intensified
> still further in undertaking to control new hazards. The
> polarity of subject and object began to develop, and with
> it the fateful obligation to form expectations based on
> necessarily insufficient evidence (*Personal Knowledge,* p.
> 388).

Once formed, and with the availability of language, such expectations are inevitably articulated and just as inevitably
passed along for the benefit of others. Teilhard has spoken of
his own "irrepressible urge to *universalize* whatever I love" (*The

Heart of Matter, 1978, p. 77). Having seen the light, one cannot but wish that others would see it too, particularly when these others are one's progeny. The wish is not entirely selfish; it is not as if we believe we have the only truth. We wish to share with others the lessons we have learned from experience so as to spare them pain; we wish their lives to be enriched as we believe ours to have been enriched by the moments of contact with greatness which our culture has offered.

Culture arises through contact between our intelligence and the natural world. It presents to us a further world of universal aspirations, of lessons not so immediate and therefore not as indubitable as our animal nature provides, but mediated through the experience of the race. Evolution represents a long chain of achievements. We have a distinguished inheritance, going back to the first moments of life. Only in accepting a role in expanding the noosphere do we adequately express this inheritance. Our model in this acceptance will surely be such a man as Pierre Teilhard de Chardin.

Spontaneity

To the therapeutic psychologists, it is as if only the spontaneous can be trusted. If something can be shown to have been *learned* (particularly under authority) it cannot be authentic. But spontaneity, Teilhard suggests, is the animal principle, no less necessary to man for that but still not representative of the highest attainment of evolution.

> For enormous periods the earth certainly lacked any real manifestation of life. Then for another enormous period in the layer of organic matter which appeared on its solid or watery envelope, it presented only signs of spontaneity, and unreflective consciousness (the animal feels and perceives; but he does not appear to know that he feels and perceives). Finally, in a relatively recent epoch, spontaneity and consciousness acquired on earth, in the zone of life that had become human, the property of isolating and individualizing themselves in their own right. Man knows that he knows. He emerges from his

actions. He dominates them in however feeble a way. He can therefore abstract, combine and foresee. He reflects. He thinks. (*The Vision of the Past*, 1966, p. 161)

How do our powers of thought develop? Not automatically. With the rise of man evolution has become conscious; we bear our responsibility for continuing the ascendant arc. Teilhard's own vocation is an example. It is doubtful his line of thought would have come into being without the thoughtful influence of his immediate progenitors:

> The spark, through which "my Universe," as yet but *half* personalized *was to attain centricity by being amorized,* that spark undoubtedly came to me through my mother: it was through her that it reached me from the current of Christian mysticism and both illuminated and inflamed my childish soul (*The Heart of Matter*, 1978, p. 41).

Our own inquiries concerning child development within the family favor the view that vocation will always bear the imprint of earliest upbringing. The suggestion is that, in the case of development within the noosphere, evolution will be carried forward through the transmission of culture. Our capacity to want and reason to what is best for our progeny is the necessary vehicle for the continuation of evolution once self-conscious beings have emerged. In recommending that parents withhold their influence in the name of their children's freedom, the therapeutic psychologists are asking that the next step of evolutionary development be a step backward.

A Practical Program for the Transmission of Ideals

We do not have adequate contemporary models of parental courage. At least in much of the psychological literature, parents who make a point of teaching their own values to their children are characterized as repressive or as fearful of change.

Concerned that the lessons of the therapists were being overgeneralized, the staff of the Center for Studies of the Person has developed a new program to investigate how the introduction of young people into the noosphere might be handled in other relational settings than psychotherapy. We have chosen to study contemporary families that work together, in which the matter of introducing children to the larger world and its lessons is a practical necessity. We call these "enterprising families" and believe they may provide a useful model of how values can be taught without heavy-handedness or preachiness—even in the face of parental timidity. What follows is an argument for the virtues of family enterprise and for the necessity of the extension of its attitudes about children to other social settings. I shall then conclude briefly with the connection between the work of the new Center for Enterprising Families and the vision of Pierre Teilhard de Chardin.

The Development of Talent

Suzuki, the Japanese violin teacher who has brought many young children to musical artistry, has said of talent that it isn't so much a native gift as it is a function of repeated contact with the world. Talent means having an absorbing interest or obligation. One tends to repeat tasks which absorb him. When one repeats them often enough, then one becomes talented. The purpose of the Suzuki program, which he calls "talent education," is to develop, in his words, "nobility of character." Youngsters are drawn into repeated contact with the world of music through the example of their parents and the shared musical occasions the system provides. Suzuki requires lessons for children to begin with lessons for their mothers. Like the Christian mysticism which amorized Teilhard's life, music is a world the child enters at the side of his mother.

Suzuki's program has spread from Japan to America and many other countries. America is no exception in being a nation settled and developed by its families. Achievement was always centered in the home. That is where time and economic advantage lay. It is still true in the performing arts. Think of the circus. Children of the circus can perform remarkable acrobatic feats—because their families routinely do them for a living. No more powerful learning center exists than the home—when the incentives are right.

We need fresh acknowledgment of the importance of family

enterprise. I define as enterprising those activities of the family which entail responsibilities to a larger community, by which the family tries to wrest reinforcement from the community. When the family organizes to meet a real-world need, the world in turn holds the family to account. Good work is expected. The family must produce.

The family farm is the best example. Nature demands that seed be placed in the ground and crops harvested on a strict schedule. And nature is unforgiving. But by meeting her demands successfully, the family gains a sense of itself as a worthwhile unit in harmony with the community. Members gain in self-respect.

In sharing responsibility for a work, family members become useful to one another in ways that otherwise are unavailable within the family, particularly to young people today. In the family enterprise, it becomes clear that everyone's effort is needed. This gives young people a sense of importance, the absence of which, I believe, is a major cause of the growing incidence of youth crime.

There is little doubt that many young people are adrift. They feel unneeded. This sad state of affairs must be reversed. If the family doesn't find a respected place for its young people, who will? The years of early adolescence have become the "useless years." The young person is not yet wanted outside the home (who will hire a thirteen-year-old girl?) but has lost her childhood identification with the family. This uselessness is a barrier to the development of the youngster. Through the criminal turn of youthful alienation in recent years, it is destructive to us all.

A Moral Vacuum
Dr. Roy Menninger, president of the Menninger Foundation, recently commented on the increasing number of young people who have "come to the Menninger Foundation for treatment and appear to have basic problems in attaining and maintaining good, constructive relationships with other people. They seem not to have learned this at home." Parents and children are no longer mutually involved. "One-parent

families are quite common, and even if there are two parents in a family, economic pressures often demand that both work. I am concerned about the divisive pressures this is exerting on families."

"Circumstances no longer throw the family together," notes philosopher Michael Novak. "The structures of American life are centrifugal, driving families apart." The society provides separate activities for male children and female children, separate activities for male parents and female parents. When family members finally get home, television takes over. "We have made television an almost universal baby-sitter," says Menninger. "We have fallen into the assumption that children raise themselves."

The rate of change in moral values has been rapid. There are now more than a million teenage pregnancies a year. A national survey recently published by Johns Hopkins researchers reported a 30-percent increase in teenage sexual activity in only five years. Twenty-five percent of young women had been initiated into sex by age sixteen; 40 percent by age seventeen.

"Why the pressure for earlier and earlier sex?" asked a *New York Times* writer who interviewed teenagers in San Francisco's Marin County. "It's just so easy," he learned. "Most homes are vacant much of the time. Mothers go to work or to their tennis clubs. Very often they are single and out on dates. Divorce is more the rule than the exception, and divorced parents, vying for the affection of their children and overtly preoccupied with sex themselves, are in no position to offer strictures. In such households, a young woman said, it's not uncommon now for high school couples to have sleep-over dates."

The statistics on juvenile crime are staggering. From 1960 to 1977 the rate of such crime rose twice as fast as the adult crime rate. More than half of all serious crimes in the U. S. are now committed by youngsters age ten to seventeen. Last year, the National Education Association estimates, nearly 61,000 teachers were attacked by students. Since 1972, classroom murders have increased 18 percent, rapes 40 percent, and assaults 72 percent.

The causes of juvenile crime are many, but a growing body of opinion holds that chief among them is the failure of the family to provide guidance for its young. Notes an experienced juvenile court judge who hears 1,000 delinquency cases a year: "The old saws about the family are true. We look for quick solutions, but family stability is the long-term answer." A recent report of the Los Angeles County Grand Jury, asserting that there is "no correlation between the rate of crime and the vast efforts to combat it via deterrent, treatment and diversion programs," urged that "the only long-range hope" for coping with juvenile crime is a renewed commitment to the teaching of values in the home.

Howard University's Samuel L. Woodard studied twenty-four Washington, D.C., junior high youngsters, each of whom had at least one parent missing, whose family income was below the poverty level, who lived in substandard housing—and yet had a record of solid academic achievement. He concluded that the common factor in these youngsters' triumph over adversity was strong family identification. "They have a sense of their families as worthwhile and valuable, even in the face of deprivation," wrote columnist William Raspberry of Woodard's research subjects. "They are required from their earliest years to meet high standards, and, as a result, come to set high standards for themselves."

Creating a Family Culture
Our minds do not develop from internal centers alone. The same need for a stimulating culture framework and the setting of high standards exists in the case of moral development as for intellectual growth. The contrary view, which I have identified with the "humanistic therapists," favors a hands-off environment, in which youngsters make their own choices and superintend their own development. That position may be appropriate to the limited treatment of cases of arrested psychological development. But when applied to normal development it fails to appreciate that the direction of growth is strongly influenced by the possibilities encouraged within the local culture. No less is "hands off" a local culture than the

"close-knit families with more supervision" which sociologists have noted among, say, the Chinese. The choice is not between freedom for the child on the one hand and parental influence on the other, but between two kinds of influence, responsible or distracted. The parent who pursues personal goals while leaving the child's moral development to the child influences his child's future profoundly. It is time to acknowledge again that human parents are capable of responsible selection of the kinds of influences to be brought to bear on their young.

Families that are without the support for high standards of traditional ethnic cultures must create their own culture through a program of shared activities within the family, particularly those which are other-centered. The father of one family performing group comments: "Our work has given me the chance to teach values without being arbitrary or preachy. For example, when I wanted our children to think about generosity, I didn't have to bring it up out of the blue. When we were asked to do a benefit performance and the children resisted, I had the opening I needed to share with them the practical importance of giving something back to the community."

The modern, sensitive parent may hesitate to insist on his values, for the reasons he can muster to support them are not likely to be as deep as the values themselves. His reasons are likely to strike the children as phony. But the richer the family's life and the more extensive its mutual involvements, the greater will be the value exemplifications in its daily affairs and the more solid the moral lessons offered its young.

The Difficulty and Necessity of Moral Lessons

For the family unable to draw connections between work and life, moral lessons are increasingly difficult to justify. We are conditioned not to accept secondhand judgments. There is no longer a parallel in the moral sphere to the necessary acceptance of tradition which provides, for example, for the continuing progress of science. Contemporary moral exploration is anarchic, each person making his own judgments. Among skill groups and professions, however, traditional techniques and values continue to be honored, as are masters, even as members strive to exceed them. It was in part through youthful involvement in work groups that youngsters were introduced to the world of values in the past. It is worth focusing on the possibilities of such a system for the guidance of young people today. Few other sources of moral education are available.

Although it has been a long time since people expected the family to produce, there are still tasks today nobody can do better than the family—and new ones appearing all the time. Our surveys indicate successful working families in every line of endeavor, in every part of the country. Living together gives the family a tremendous advantage, when they use it.

We should encourage more families to bind themselves. We should bring to light the existing examples of family enterprise in every community. Such families represent the beginnings of an international network of great good example. We should encourage the development of more family enterprises. Among its other virtues, it is a marvelous vehicle for cross-generational bonding. In working together, important values are exemplified for both generations. Differences between them are eased.

Inserting the World into the Child-Rearing Equation

The temper of the times is that it is hard for one individual to subordinate himself to another. We have been living in the day of "me first."

The young members of a family performing group are seen helping unload the band truck, carrying instruments into the hall; older ones setting them up for younger. The mother comments: "These are children who resist helping with dishes at home, who, no matter how often I holler at them, leave their rooms in a mess."

But on the job they help. Why? "Maybe it has to do with the applause, people's interest in them, the pride they take in helping support the family, even the chance to give good service. They know that if we are to give a decent performance, the supporting work must be done. They can see there's more than their father and I can handle alone. Besides, it would look bad if they let us do it all. They know that."

At home no one sees except the family. There's no embarrassment in that. A child's room is in a mess. "Yeah, Mom, but who's going to see my room?"

The children of working families develop publicly identifiable skills. Society rewards their efforts with attention and often more tangible considerations. The child is reinforced in part for his family membership but also for what he achieves individually. The band father notes that "Our children have trouble, as I suppose many do today, subordinating themselves to their parents. They have the independence appropriate to these times." But they can subordinate themselves to a real-world purpose. "They love applause. They like earning money."

Applause and money are the kinds of real-world reinforcers that will bring an adult to self-discipline. In working families they or their equivalents are available to the child as well. In too many contemporary child-rearing schemes the contingencies are solely between the child and the parent. They are, if you will, too personal to be effective today.

Teilhard has shown us that our transcendence is to be found in and through the world. More youngsters would be seen to exercise self-discipline if the world more often entered into the child-rearing equation. Such discipline is not an end in itself. It is rather a stepping-stone to the attainment of higher ideals. We live in a time in evolutionary history when our opportunity is to participate more fully in the spiritual realities toward which the world is being drawn. Such a time is not one for timidity on the part of parents. We must be like Teilhard's own mother, unself-conscious about our influence, helping to start our children on a further journey toward what we have learned is good and true.

On the occasion of their wedding in 1948, Teilhard spoke to his young friends Christine Dresch and Claude Marie Haardt. He urged them to fix their eyes "on what is greater and finer than you" and to forgo the temptation of "shared selfishness . . . which besets love . . . and makes it barren."

To find one another, and to be truly made one, you must
seek no other road but that of a strong passion for a
common Ideal. Between the two of you (and here the
very structure of the world forces upon you a law that
cannot be broken)—between the two of you, remember,
no unblemished union can exist except in some higher
center which brings you together (*The Heart of Matter*,
1978, p. 151).

He goes on to urge that such a center will be found in their
children. The law of evolution is that parents will be drawn
further toward the ideal through the spiritual achievements of
their progeny. But these children must have a base. They must
not be denied their inheritance—in all its particularity—
through parental suspicion that experts know better. Such
"knowing better" is often abstract, a transfer from an appropriate to an inappropriate context. First we must plant our feet
firmly if we are to spring toward the light. The world in which
we gather our resources is the concrete world in which we find
ourselves. It is not a world of abstract expertise.

Works Referred to in the Text

Gordon, Thomas. *Parent Effectiveness Training*. New York: New
    American Library, 1970.

Polanyi, Michael. *Personal Knowledge*. Chicago: University of Chicago
    Press, 1958.

————."Scientific Thought and Social Reality: Essays by Michael
    Polanyi." *Psychological Issues*, vol. 8, no. 4. New York: International
    Universities Press, 1974.

Teilhard de Chardin, Pierre. *The Future of Man*. New York: Harper &
    Row, 1964.

————. *The Heart of Matter*. New York: Harcourt Brace Jovanovich,
    1978.

————. *The Vision of the Past*. New York: Harper & Row, 1966.

CHANGING VIEWS OF CREATIVITY AND EVOLUTION

Willis W. Harman

In October 1979 there was held in Cordoba, Spain, an international colloquium on "Science and Consciousness," sponsoréd by the France Culture program division of Radio France. The meeting is symbolic of where we are in history. Scholars and researchers of various nations and diverse disciplines gathered to discuss what is increasingly perceived as a core issue in today's "crisis of civilization"—the reconciliation of the two basic paths to human understanding, that of rational empirical science and that of the inner search via the mind of intuition and creative imagination.

Even a few years ago, it is hard to imagine such an assemblage of neurophysiologists, theoretical physicists, psychiatrists, psychologists (from cognitive to Jungian), parapsychologists, and religious philosophers (from East, West, and Middle East), seeking synthesis of these seemingly disparate partial looks at the phenomenon of human consciousness. Until very recently scientists showed little tendency to ask whether the experiences of the "deep intuition," that central concern of the humanities and religions, had something essential to contribute to the scientific picture of humanity-in-the-world. And religionists seemed equally unconcerned to ask whether there might be an underlying, explorable realm of human experience transcending specific religious formulations and presenting a basis for broad consensus. As for scientists and religionists to pursue their inquiries together, that seemed almost a violation of union rules.

An Emerging Contradiction

It should have been apparent long ago that the dominating knowledge system of every society—including our own—is in some sense a cultural artifact. To be sure, science differs from many of the knowledge systems of the past in its insistence on open inquiry and public validation of knowledge. Within that broad definition of science, however, the topics emphasized and not emphasized, the questions asked and not asked, are culturally influenced. Thus an industrializing society gives central attention to gaining knowledge that will generate new technologies—that will increase abilities to predict, control, and manipulate. This dominating pursuit tends to squeeze out other kinds of knowledge emphases.

Thus the industrial society of a half century ago found itself almost convinced that what is measurable is what is real, and that our most direct experience—that of conscious awareness—is somehow less real and less worthy of study than that which can be expressed in quantified terms. We found ourselves confused about eternal values and enduring goals; with ever-more-powerful "know-how" and growing unsureness about what is ultimately worth doing. The materialistic preoccupations of scientists, combined with their high prestige, led to doubt of a most fundamental sort—doubt that religion, morality, and the human being's power to make free choices are more than figments of the imagination, and that Western man, traditionally endowed with reason, will, and a valid sense of value, is anything but an exploded myth.

There was an unnoticed contradiction here. The popular impact of science was to cast doubt on the validity of creative insight and intuitive sense of what is right. Yet at the same time the whole history of science is of intuitive leaps substantiated by laborious and methodical testing of the intuitively arrived-at hypotheses. The motivation of science, in fact, is strongly rooted in an intuitive faith that the universe is ultimately understandable by methods of systematic inquiry. As for involvement with value issues, the most telling example in all of science is probably the area of psychosomatic illness and placebo effect. There is now compelling evidence that illness—both stress diseases and those due to external pathogens normally warded off by the body's immune system—is profoundly affected by attitudes. Thus some attitudes—e.g., resentment, anxiety—are unwholesome in that they contribute to illness; other attitudes—e.g., joy, love, humor—are wholesome in that they foster healing and wellness. But attitudes are directly related to beliefs. Thus some beliefs are demonstrably unwholesome and other beliefs are wholesome. That is a pretty far-reaching value statement! It seems especially so when one considers the evidence that basic cultural premises underlying modern industrial civilization are of questionable wholesomeness for either persons or the planet.

Teilhard de Chardin is perhaps the person who has made the greatest single contribution toward calling this contradiction to our attention. Nothing represents so well as Teilhard's differences with his own church the uneasy relationship between institutionalized religion and institutionalized science, and the equally uneasy relationship between either and the maverick who dares to explore outside the accepted conceptual frameworks and paradigms. Yet the great reconciliation which Teilhard's work symbolizes seems now finally to be taking place. To illustrate the sea change occurring in the cultural and intellectual milieu I would like to focus on the concepts of *evolution* and *creativity*.

Changing Fashions in Knowledge

After the 17th-century tacit "division of labor" between the tender new scientific societies and the powerfully entrenched religious institutions (wherein the physically measurable realm of human experience was appropriated by the former and the mental and spiritual largely left to the latter), various boundary areas became scenes of jurisdictional conflict. Among these, two in particular became crucial intellectual battlegrounds.

They were the creation and/or evolution of humankind and the nature of the "deep intuition." The latter was referred to in the 19th century through terms like "soul," "inspiration," and "conscience"; by the late 20th century one was much more likely to hear the words "creativity" and "intuition" to point tentatively in the same general direction.

These two issues—creativity and evolution—had been closely related in the religious mind, in that the same Divine Mind responsible for the creation/evolution of the universe was the Source of inspiration and the Inner Voice of conscience. However by the first half of the 20th century the prevailing scientific view of evolution had become a story of the random assembling of complex life-creating molecules, followed by eons of random mutations and random sorting out of those forms better fit to survive. The development of human consciousness had come about by a succession of accidents. Similarly, the prevailing view of conscience had become Freud's superego—the introjected parent and internalized social dictates, ruling the person through moral attitudes and a sense of guilt. As for "inspiration," the connotations of the word had become embarrassing and its surrogate "creativity" was much preferred, tending to connote the spewing out of lucky patterns by the operations of a fantastically complex digital computer in the brain. The "war between science and religion" was essentially over; the battles of Darwinism and Freudianism had been won by science and there remained little doubt about the ultimate outcome. Empirical science had replaced doctrinal religion as the ultimate authority on the interpretation of human experience. Henceforth experience relating to human consciousness would be "explained" in terms of measurable parameters of the central nervous system.

Then a remarkable thing happened on the way to the future. Human consciousness began to come back as an empirical (or at least existential) fact of human existence. First in the culture, then on the fringes of academic science, questions began to be raised about the peculiarity of industrial culture that seemed to deny the existence of that which had been held to be centrally important in practically ever traditional culture on the globe—human consciousness and the human spirit.

British physicist Sir Arthur Eddington had many years ago told of the icthyologist who, after combing the seas with a net of one-inch mesh, arrived at the "scientific" conclusion that there are no creatures in the sea with a diameter less than one inch. The quantitative emphasis of most contemporary science, tending to equate what is physically measurable with what is "real," is like the one-inch-mesh net. It captures some aspects of reality and misses others. Lord Kelvin's dictum, that only if you can measure it can you talk about it, would have to be replaced by the criterion of the French poet Saint-Exupéry: "Truth is not that which is demonstrable. Truth is that which is *ineluctable"*— that which cannot be escaped.

Three Types of Knowledge

In our attempt to understand this peculiar omission of modern scientific knowledge it will be helpful to compare three types of knowledge systems, especially as they relate to human consciousness. Different societies have had differing dominant knowledge systems, depending on their emphasis on the various uses for that knowledge. Let us contrast three imaginary knowledge systems with three quite different emphases on intended use. Depending on whether the predominant focus is on knowledge for *prediction and control,* knowledge *to guide human development,* or the *search for meaning,* the characteristics of the knowledge system would tend to be something as shown in the chart on page 38.

In real life these purposes overlap and there is some concern for all three emphases in every society. Nevertheless it seems clear that there are significant differences between societies. For example, the knowledge system of the Native American Indians or of the Europeans in the Middle Ages placed preponderant emphasis on meaning, whereas modern industrial society has shaped its knowledge system to focus on increasing the ability to predict and control and to manage the environment through technology. Accompanying this emphasis of in-

A Comparison of Three Types of Knowledge Systems

Primary focus	Applications	Characteristics
Prediction and control	Develop technologies, manipulate and control the physical environment, develop and produce goods and services	Emphasis on measurable information, quantified descriptions, deterministic models, reductionistic explanations
Human development	Guide actions relating to human development, education, physical and emotional health, psychotherapy and counseling	Concern with purpose, volition; value issues; teleological explanations; models and metaphors involving holistic concepts; explorations of alternative states of consciousness
Meaning	Psychotherapy and counseling; religion	Concern with meaning, ultimate goals; alternative states of consciousness, especially "deep intuition"

dustrial society has come a tendency to treat the other kinds of knowledge as inferior or unimportant. Thus, for example, purpose and meaning are not concepts that refer directly to things that are physical and measurable. They are awkward for contemporary science to deal with, and have been largely relegated to the humanities and to religion. But along with that consignment went the implication that since science didn't deal with purpose and meaning (other than as idiosyncratic notions that could be explained in terms of more measurable—hence "real"—causes) they must be either illusory or unimportant.

Surely one of the great advances of human civilization, by

almost any criteria, must be the idea of science—the democratization and refinement of knowledge through the principles of open inquiry and public validation. There is no apparent reason to doubt that science in this broad sense is equally applicable to all three of the above knowledge foci. We have already indicated that there would be significant differences between a science focused on prediction and control; and systematized knowledge gathered around the question of human development, or the question of meaning. For example, in the former there is great emphasis on reliable data through replicable experiment. On the other hand, to understand human development requires exploration of exceptional human capabilities. Here volition is an integral part of the exceptional actualization of potentialities. It should not be surprising if these exceptional capacities (e.g., extrasensory perception) seem in conflict with models of reality constructed from the prediction-and-control emphasis. Or considering another example, the ways used to consensually validate the knowledge about our deepest goal commitments coming from explorations of "deep intuition" (i.e., states of consciousness referred to in mystical and religious literature) will be quite different from the comparison of quantified physical measurements characteristic of the prediction-and-control focus. The human mind is the instrument of observation, and it must meet certain conditions to enable it to observe with clarity (e.g., nonattachment to ego goals). Taking such differences into account, it seems that one day we will have global consensus regarding the other two foci in the same way that we presently have near global consensus regarding prediction-and-control science.

Conscious and Unconscious Knowing

Anticipating such an expanded development of our knowledge system I would like to conjecture how we might come to look at the two topics creativity and evolution, extrapolating from established research findings and the results of exploratory investigations. A good starting place is the broad finding, by now firmly established, that much of our mental activity goes on outside conscious awareness. In fact it seems that only the most minute part of our total mental activity is in that narrow "visible spectrum" between the "infrared" of the subconscious (e.g., instinctual drives, repressed memories, autonomic functioning) and the "ultraviolet" of the supraconscious (e.g., creative imagination, intuitive judgment, aesthetic sense).

Some of this "out-of-consciousness" activity is, so to speak, in the "deep unconscious" and we become aware of it only through inference. Some of it, at another extreme, is at least partly accessible to conscious awareness under certain conditions—e.g., through hypnotic suggestion, biofeedback training, meditation, autogenic training and other self-regulatory exercises, and sensory deprivation.

One of the most important discoveries relating to this is the phenomenon of "unconscious knowing." In biofeedback training, for example, the individual finds that unconsciously he "knows" how to dilate capillaries and change blood flow in his fingertip, to relax muscle tensions causing headaches, to change brainwave patterns and accompanying subjective states. Without the feedback signal (e.g., reading of a temperature sensor on the fingertip) the person doesn't know he knows (e.g., how to change the blood flow).

A familiar example of this unconscious knowing relates closely to creativity. This is the calling up of a forgotten name. We see a familiar face but the person's name eludes us. The more we strain the more elusive it is. Finally we "file a request" with that "other part" of the mind to please come up with the name, and go on to think about other things. Then perhaps in the middle of a conversation, or a game of golf, or a nap, up pops the name. Unconsciously we know how to search the memory files; consciously we don't know how we do it. The mind that knows how I will refer to here as the creative/intuitive mind.

Business executives, architects, inventors, poets, artists, composers, scientists, all have repeatedly told of experiences with the problem-solving ability of this creative/intuitive mind. Insight seems to come from some behind-the-scenes creative process, often after the conscious mind has wrestled with a problem and "tried everything," and often when the conscious mind is distracted from the problem. Sometimes the answer is put forth in easily recognizable form; sometimes in veiled imagery. Sometimes it is visual; sometimes auditory; sometimes simply as a sure inner knowing. The solutions typically not only "feel" right but test out in application.

It seems to be true that the more we believe in the abilities of this "other part" of our minds, the more we use it and have faith in it, the better it performs. In fact it appears that the greatest single obstacle to expanded use of the creative/intuitive mind is lack of consistent belief in its abilities. Research ranging from laboratory studies of hypnosis to fieldwork in cultural anthropology, from experiments on expectation set to psychotherapy, from the placebo effect to psychological consequences of cosmetic surgery, all points to one conclusion: The power of attitudes, beliefs, suggestion, and image to influence perception, behavior, manifest capabilities, and health, is far greater than is typically considered to be the case.

The power of suggestion is most vividly demonstrated in phenomena related to hypnosis. Hypnotic suggestion can profoundly affect the way I perceive the world, or the way I behave and the abilities I can manifest. But hypnosis is in one sense a very simple phenomenon. It requires but that I be open to suggestion and that there be a source of suggestion, external or internal. These conditions are met in each one of us from infancy—we are open, and we are surrounded by people eager to suggest to us how we should perceive the world. Thus our perceptions of ourselves and our potentialities are strongly affected by suggestions we unwittingly picked up in infancy—by a sort of "cultural hypnosis." This observation is not new—a host of sages from Socrates to Ouspensky have insisted that we are hypnotized from infancy, and that the central task of adult life is to "know thyself," become "dehypnotized" or "enlightened."

Hiding our Creative Selves

A part of the "unconscious knowing" is clearly knowing how to hide from myself. One part of myself represses, hides things

from another part of myself, including that most vital knowledge of my own identity and potentialities. Maslow referred to
this fundamental ambivalence about knowing in a chapter title
in *Towards a Psychology of Being:* "On the Need to Know and the
Fear of Knowing." He noted that we do indeed, as is well
known, fear to know the unsavory about ourselves which we
have carefully repressed. But, he said, even more do we fear to
know our highest potentialities, "the godlike in ourselves."

We think we want to see reality as it is and ourselves as we
are—to see truthfully. But the illusions we have are part of an
unconsciously held belief system; any attack on those illusions
is perceived (unconsciously) as a threat. Thus an effort to dispel
illusion, though ultimately beneficial, may nevertheless generate resistance. We truly desire to discover and actualize our
highest creative/intuitive capabilities. Yet to the extent that re-
moving illusion, "dehypnotizing," is essential to that discovery,
we will resist that which we truly desire. We may, in fact, resist it
using the most convincing "scientific" arguments and concepts,
"proving" to ourselves that the creative/intuitive mind *must* be
limited in the information to which it has access, or the kinds of
solutions it could conceivably bring forth.

The relevance of this observation to creativity becomes apparent when we consider one specific implication of the creative experience. As mentioned earlier, the more "belief in" the
creative/intuitive mind the more effective it seems to be. There
are no clear limits on the potentialities of this creative unconscious "higher" mind. That being the case, if it seems to be so
much more knowledgeable and wise than one's conscious rational mind; if it has access to all the knowledge available to
consciousness and more; then the clear implication is that one
should not stop at submitting to it only the specific problems
that the ego-mind has selected out as "difficult." It is not
marked "For emergency use only." Why not turn to it with *all*
decisions, including the most important and the most immediate: What should I do next moment? What should I do
with the rest of my life?

But the ego-mind is not eager to lose its control and become
subservient to the creative/intuitive mind. It does not want to

admit the belief that a "higher" mind exists, and it assembles its most logical arguments to disprove the possibility. An important step in freeing up the creative/intuitive mind is recognition of this resistance.

There are two major arguments supporting this idea that the creative/intuitive mind be given charge of all choices, however large or small. One is that this is the recommendation at the core of most if not all spiritual traditions, representing the accumulated experience of many generations of seers and inner explorers. The other reason is that while science does not demonstrate the idea, many of its findings point in that direction or are at least compatible with it.

The "Perennial Wisdom"

Comparative examination of the rich variety of religious traditions in human history leads to an important conclusion that can be stated in two parts:

1. The religious beliefs and practices of a culture tend to fall into two parts, an *exoteric* or public version, and an *esoteric* version understood by some inner circle and tending to require for its understanding a rigorous discipline involving some sort of exploration or extraordinary states of consciousness.

2. Although the exoteric versions differ markedly, one from the other, the esoteric versions appear to be essentially the same for all durable traditions, East and West, ancient and modern, primitive and sophisticated.* This conclusion implies that all these traditions are rooted in the same kind of deep inner experience, potentially accessible to all humans.

This "perennial wisdom" at the core of the world's spiritual traditions includes something like the following propositions:

A. Each of us is culturally hypnotized from infancy, perceiving the world the way we have been hypnotized to perceive it. A

---

* This point is made by numerous scholars. One excellent source is Whitall Perry, *A Treasury of Traditional Wisdom* (Simon & Schuster, 1971). A more popular version can be found in Aldous Huxley's *The Perennial Philosophy* (Harper & Row, 1945).

prime task of adult life is to become dehypnotized, "en-lightened."

B. As this dehypnotization occurs it becomes apparent that there are potential levels of consciousness far beyond ordinary consciousness in the sense that ordinary consciousness is beyond dreamless sleep. These levels may sporadically become accessible to conscious awareness. They include the creative/intuitive mind, whose contents seep through into conscious awareness as creative problem solutions, moral insight, or artistic inspiration. Ecological, humane, and spiritual value commitments are all rooted in this realm of human experience.

C. Access to this higher mind can be improved by reinforcing one's belief in it, and through practicing nonattachment to all else. In the end, one discovers it to be capable of guiding us far more reliably than the conscious analytical ego-mind.

D. The central understanding coming from this realm of experience is that there is one Mind of which we all partake. Thus mind is in no way limited, as a physical model of the brain-mind would suggest—in extensibility in space or time, in separateness from other minds or from nature, in the potentiality of creating effects in the physical world.

E. Thus, at the deepest level, all people share a common interest and a common destiny—a destiny that far transcends the greed and fear, the pain and conflict, around which so much of our society is constructed.

Extrapolations from Scientific Findings

The second kind of argument for entrusting decisions to the creative/intuitive mind comes from extrapolation of scientific findings, particularly those relating to unconscious processes and those from parapsychology (psychic research). The findings of psychic research, particularly those on remote viewing (clairvoyant perception) and on precognition and retrocognition, indicate that effects of mind are not limited by distance of physical time in ways that conventional views would suggest.

Rather, mind exists in coextensive unity with the world it observes.

From research on the power of beliefs and expectations to shape perceptions we can conclude that the belief that minds are separate from one another (common enough in our culture) puts limitations on belief in the potentialities of the creative/intuitive mind, and that in turn limits access to the creative/intuitive mind.

Recent research on telepathic communication reinforces the conclusion that we have knowledge of what is going on in other minds, even when this knowledge is not accessible to conscious awareness. (In one such experiment a flashing strobe light stimulus in one person's eyes produces an electrical component in the EEG pattern of another, distant and isolated, who is not consciously aware of whether the remote strobe light is flashing or not.) The implication of such research is that individuals' minds are in continuous communication in ways not accounted for by subliminal sounds, visual cues, or other physical sensory signals.

If minds are joined, the knowledge potentially available to an individual mind is much greater than if minds were separate. More importantly, the kind of problem-solution to be expected is qualitatively different. If our minds are part of a "collective supraconscious mind" then my ultimate well-being is not separate from that of my neighbor.

It is not even necessary to exclude interactions between mind and the physical world. Psychokinetic phenomena recently studied include moving objects, producing images on photographic film, changing temperature, and affecting magnetometer readings, apparently from concentration of the mind alone without physical mechanisms of any known type. A few extraordinary persons, down through the centuries, have been reported as able to perform such phenomena. Now it appears likely it will turn out that, as with the fingertip blood flow example mentioned earlier, we all "know" unconsciously how to produce all these phenomena—but we don't *know* we know unless sensitive feedback is provided.

A word has to be said about the hazard of "listening" to the wrong "inner voice." The religious traditions spoken of earlier have all urged the importance of testing what may seem to be the promptings of the creative/intuitive mind. One way is to check with tradition, with the insights of those who have gone before. Another is to note that the right kind of "listening" will tend to increase closeness with others. There is some risk in making the attempt to listen to the "inner voice"; there is far more ultimate risk in not doing so.

One of the key conditions, both for increasing access to the higher mind and for avoiding distortion of the "inner voice" is nonattachment to all other goals, ambitions, desires. Traditionally, one of the powerful techniques for arriving at this nonattachment is through autosuggestion; recent research on hypnosis tends to substantiate how powerfully this technique can affect the unconscious mind.

An Observation about Evolution

We have explored the phenomena of creativity and seen that the direction pointed to by modern science appears to be quite compatible with that of the "perennial wisdom." With that background in mind, let us make a few observations about our second theme: evolution.

Until recently, acceptable explanations for evolutionary developments tended to be quite mechanistic. Take, for example, the question of how in the evolutionary process we ended up with two eyes and binocular vision. The acceptable sort of explanation tended to speak of things like random mutations, the accidental appearance of an organism with rudimentary binocular vision, enhanced survival capabilities because of improved vision, natural selection—and so we all have two eyes! Although this kind of explanation left a tremendous lot to "accident," it nonetheless was the explanation most students were expected to accept.

There is another kind of explanation that suggests itself once the presence of a higher mind is recognized to be not so contradictory to science as was once thought. That other kind of explanation speaks of some sort of teleological "pull" in the evolutionary process; of evolution toward increased awareness, complexity, freedom; in short, of evolution *going somewhere.* In that kind of evolutionary explanation the organism developed two eyes because it wanted to see better! The long path of evolutionary development is not so much pushed by random mutations and natural selection as it is pulled by a higher consciousness. In this kind of explanation mind is prior to brain, and evolution is characterized both by the organism's freedom to choose and by its inner sense of a preferred direction. This has been a totally unacceptable form of explanation in modern sophisticated circles—yet it is much more in tune with the "perennial wisdom" and much more congenial to the sense among a growing group of scientists that consciousness somehow has to be factored into our total picture of the universe.

We aren't there yet—the great reconciliation Teilhard envisioned has not yet happened. But perhaps we aren't as far from it as is generally thought to be the case.

LITERACY, EVOLUTION, AND DEVELOPMENT

Robert A. Rubinstein and Sol Tax

The ability to read and write is unique to the human species, yet not all people *can* read and write; many are illiterate. This is so despite the fact that for decades colonial and indigenous governments, international agencies, and grass-roots organizations have all put forth major efforts to develop successful literacy programs. Together with a reading of the literacy literature, this leaves the impression that adult literacy programs have not been particularly successful. At the very least, it can be said, the acquisition and maintenance of literacy skills by adults is extremely difficult. Why is that? Despite much work, the reasons for the difficulty are poorly understood by behavioral scientists and educators. In this essay we look at some of the consequences of being illiterate, set out our view of what might be learned from the examination of one kind of reading disorder about the possible neurological basis of literacy, and offer some initial speculations about literacy and human evolution.

We take up this topic as our contribution to this volume marking the one-hundredth anniversary of the birth of Teilhard de Chardin because it involves the development of an understanding of one of the processes in human evolution through which human beings are continually expanding their capacity to store and manipulate information about objects and relationships in space and time that are beyond those immediately obvious to their senses. And because the implications for the design of literacy training that derive from this understanding are just one example of how people participate directly in setting the course of human evolution. Both of these concerns were major themes in Teilhard's work and his hopes for the future.

To those who have grown up as members of a society where most adults can read and write at least simple messages, reading seems a very natural and, indeed, even an easy process. While many may recall some of the initial difficulties they experienced as children when they first learned to read, they no longer remember in detail the process of learning to read. It now seems completely natural to pick up a newspaper and read about the day's events with relatively little effort. We see printed symbols and derive from them linguistic meaning. To be unable to do this seems a tremendous handicap. Literacy becomes a valued end in itself. To people who participate in literate societies, it may be surprising to learn that major portions of the world are largely illiterate (for example, in some African and Asian countries nine out of ten adults cannot read or write), and that UNESCO now estimates that more than 814 million people, aged fifteen or over, can neither read nor write.

The storage and transmission of knowledge through written media have real consequences for social organization and social action. After all, writing provides an extremely efficient system for storing and manipulating information about all aspects of human life. Once acquired, writing changes the nature of people's participation in their society. As Jack Goody and Ian Watt pointed out, when a society begins to record its history in a written medium, the nature of the individuals' access to their cultural tradition changes.

In "preliterate" societies cultural traditions are transmitted through face-to-face interactions. During this interaction people tend to change the collective memory of their society; inconsistencies between beliefs about the past and about how the present should be, and the reality of the present, are eliminated as the tradition is continually reworked in everyday conversations. Goody and Watt argue that this leads to a situation of "structural amnesia" in which disagreement with the view of the past offered by tradition leads to noncumulative, personal skepticism. That is, it "does not lead to a deliberate rejection and reinterpretation of social dogma so much as to a semiautomatic readjustment of belief." [1]

When a society becomes literate it gives up the luxury of this easy mechanism for the nondisruptive redefinition of itself. Because writing provides a more efficient system for preserving its "history," discontinuities between accurate records of the past and the society's story about the past accumulate. As a result, social dogma is not readjusted, and members may be faced with mounting numbers of inconsistencies in, and contradictions to, the cultural tradition.

Literacy, then, has two faces. It provides the means for storing and manipulating ever-growing bodies of general information and specialized knowledge about the world. It means, as well, that a society trades off this ability against a potential for the easy maintenance of a sense of cultural continuity. Indeed, it is this trade-off that provides one of the motivations for the development of literacy.

Until 1819, when the 85-character syllabary for Cherokee was developed in its "final" form by Sequoya, the Cherokee Nation was almost totally illiterate. Almost overnight, it seems, the Cherokee became a literate society. Just eleven years later, in 1830, fully 50 percent of the adult population was able to read and write in the Cherokee language.

Between 1828, when the Cherokee began publishing their own Cherokee-language newspaper (and, shortly thereafter, books and other materials), and the early twentieth century the Cherokee sustained a literate society, though it never fully regained its earlier vigor after the Cherokee press was disrupted by the Civil War. In 1963, when Sol Tax began to direct a Carnegie Corporation-funded project in cross-cultural education among the Cherokee of eastern Oklahoma, the tribe was again mostly illiterate, both in Cherokee and in English.

The development and decline of literacy among the Cherokee was dramatic; how can it be accounted for? In the early twentieth century the social context of Cherokee literacy changed significantly. In the 1800s the Cherokee were recognized as a separate nation. The printing of Cherokee-language materials (and, of course, the reading and writing of these) served as a means of validating this independent identity. Publication of a Cherokee-language newspaper allowed members of the tribe to participate in the discussion and management of the day-to-day affairs of their nation; religious tracts reinforced the traditional importance of ceremonial life among the Cherokee, and boys' and girls' seminaries, run by the Cherokee, were established to support the teaching of literacy.

In 1907 Oklahoma became a state, Congress dissolved the Cherokee Nation by formal act, and the Cherokee return to being a nonliterate society accelerated. Since the end of the Civil War the government had been slowly eroding the rights of the Cherokee, eventually placing their affairs under Federal jurisdiction. Thus, the formal dissolution of the Cherokee Nation came as the culmination of forty years of increasing pressure upon and oppression of the Cherokee. In a word, in order for the Cherokee to preserve their integrity as a culture, participation in literate society became counterproductive; the social context had changed and the motivation for literacy removed. The Cherokee began to build social and psychological walls to insulate themselves and to cut themselves off from economic, political, and social ties with the larger white society in order to ensure their identity as a people. They developed a "structural isolation" from the surrounding white society.

The Cherokee case teaches some general lessons about literacy. It demonstrates that literacy can be achieved through the spontaneous efforts of a community, without importing formal, externally designed programs. It suggests, further, that literacy is fundamentally a social, rather than an individual, achievement, deriving from a group's efforts to adapt successfully to its environment.[2]

On the face of it, perhaps, this may appear contrary to what we said at the start of this essay about the relative lack of success of adult literacy programs. In fact, it is totally consistent. Perhaps the major result of experiences with organized adult literacy programs is the knowledge that when they succeed they do so, not because being able to read and write is taken as a valued end in itself, but because reading and writing are accomplishments valued by a group because they support other socially valued undertakings.

To this point we have not defined literacy, except indirectly, by saying that literate societies are those in which most adult members can read and write at least simple messages. We think a useful distinction can be made between two qualitatively different types of reading. We call these *functional reading* and *proficient reading*, and we characterize them roughly as follows. When a person must attend to every detail of the printed page (perhaps finding changes in type style and between printing and script difficult), labors over the material before him, and reads relatively slowly, but nonetheless understands what he has read, he is performing functional reading. It is this kind of reading that is taken as a minimum threshold for saying that literacy has been attained. (This threshold is usually defined by equating it with some formal educational benchmark such as "reading at the fifth-grade level.")

Of course, this is a minimal measure, and newly literate societies may have members whose skills far outstrip these. But it is this kind of reading that is the hallmark of skills newly acquired in adult literacy classes.

The second type of reading, proficient reading, involves the development of the ability to skip and skim, to pass relatively effortlessly and quickly through most printed material, and to comprehend complex and technical writing. It is this proficient reading that characterizes the skills of many members of societies that have relatively long traditions of literacy.

These two types of reading are not mutually exclusive. In the course of developing proficient reading it is necessary that an individual first become a functional reader, though the amount of time spent as a functional reader shows great variation among proficient readers in any society. Further, it is important to recognize that some people who become functional readers never achieve proficient reading. We have drawn attention to this elementary distinction because it serves as a useful bridge between looking at the functions of literacy on the group level, as we have above, and viewing the achievement of proficient reading in individual and evolutionary perspective.

Much of what we know about the neurological basis of language has come from the study of the effects of various kinds of injury or insult to the human brain. By observing the effects of known brain traumas, or by inferring from observed changes in language behavior what neurological damage has occurred from accident or illness (and later confirming these inferences in *post mortem* examinations) we have also built up an understanding of the possible evolutionary basis of language. Although this has not been as extensively the case with reading, physicians and other researchers have observed and recorded many cases of *alexia*—the loss of the ability to read—and diagnosis of the causes of such cases has become increasingly accurate.

There are many types of alexia, depending upon what other symptoms (such as the loss of the expression and reception of spoken language) accompany the loss of reading. Norman Geschwind has been a particularly active researcher in this area. His work has done much to standardize the diagnosis of alexic conditions, to distinguish between different types of alexia, and to advance the theoretical understanding of the physiological and evolutionary basis of the alexias.[3]

During the past two years we have had the opportunity to observe closely and to question extensively an individual who suffers from alexia without agraphia, or what the clinical literature calls "pure alexia." Published descriptions of this syndrome report that it is relatively rare (perhaps representing about one of every 1,000 cases of alexia). It typically involves only the loss of the ability to read. The reception and production of spoken language is unaffected, and the alexic without agraphia can even write (hence the qualification "without agraphia")—though is not able to read what was just written!

The person with whom we have worked (VPA) is a university professor, active in his field and, like his colleagues, a voracious reader. He displays the classic pattern of alexia without agraphia described in the literature, except that he retains an ability to read at a rate of about fifty words per minute in the manner of what we described as functional reading.

A series of tests was administered to VPA when he first reported that he was having difficulty reading. The tests confirmed what he had himself reported; only his reading ability seemed to be effected, all of his other abilities were at their normal levels. VPA's physicians suspect that he had suffered a mild stroke, causing damage to specific areas of the brain.

In most people language ability is "localized" in the left hemisphere of the brain. A region of the frontal cortex, called Broca's Area, plays the significant role in the production of spoken language, while Wernicke's Area, in the temporal lobe, is critical to language comprehension. Working together, these two areas of the left hemisphere support the expression and reception of spoken language. But what about reading?

At the rear of both hemispheres of the brain, in the occipital lobe, are the areas of the brain in which visual input is analyzed. When reading, visual information is transferred from these occipital lobes to the language areas, and visual input gets translated into linguistic input. The left visual areas directly communicate with the language areas through a number of neural pathways. Before visual information input to the right occipital lobes can be translated to meaningful linguistic units, it must cross from the right into the left hemisphere. This crossing occurs through the *corpus callosum,* a large bundle of nerves that allows the left and right hemispheres to communicate with each other. A particular part at the back of the corpus callosum, the *splenium,* is the bridge over which information from the right visual area travels to reach the language area in the left hemisphere.

Reading in part depends upon the adequate functioning of each of these areas of the brain, and on the maintenance of the connections between them. In alexia without agraphia the visual-association area in the left hemisphere is damaged, and the splenium's transfer of information between the two hemispheres is somehow disrupted. The result is that letters can be viewed by the right hemisphere but this visual input cannot be passed along to and given linguistic interpretation in the left hemisphere.

We have said that in combination with a lesion in the left occipital area, the disruption of the connection provided by the splenium (between the visual areas of the two hemispheres of the brain), the ability to read is lost. This does not adequately convey the mystery of the situation. The splenium is *not* a large bundle of nerves interconnecting the two hemispheres. Rather, it is a relatively small portion of the much larger corpus callosum. When this connection is broken *only* the ability to read is lost. VPA confirms this for us; all other mental functions, memory, calculation, speech, and so on, are normal!

We think this situation most interesting. In the course of the evolution of complex organisms, many structures develop which serve more than one function. Usually it can be seen that one or more of these multiple functions are overlaid on a structure, the evolution of which was shaped by environmental pressures, and which resulted in a way of accommodating some other primary function. Consider, for example, the structure of the human hand and the visual system. The structure of the hand includes digits, which can be moved independently, as well as a thumb, which can be brought into direct opposition to the other fingers on the hand. This allows the precise movement of the fingers so that we can grasp small objects, but it allows us to firmly grasp and hold tightly to larger objects as well. The visual system is stereoscopic, achieving this effect with a structure that allows the fields of vision of the two eyes to overlap. This, in turn, functions to allow us to judge accurately distance and depth. Separately and together these structural arrangements appear to have been useful in helping hominids to better exploit the environments in which they live by functioning to allow the manipulation of objects and the facilitation of movement.

These structures also subserve other, different functions; we write, view movies, make jewelry, and so on. If we broke our thumb, and it was thus no longer opposable to our other fingers, writing or jewelry-making would become laboriously difficult activities. But it is also true that such a misfortune would make it more difficult in some other ways as well to carry on life as usual.

There is no reason to suppose that matters are any different with the structures in the brain. In fact, there is evidence that the brain is not unique; structures in the brain serve multiple functions. But this is the interesting and, we think, critical point; trauma to the splenium (in conjunction with loss of the use of the left visual area) appears to result *only* in the loss of reading ability.

The human brain probably came to have its present structure at least 100,000 years ago. It is then, in the middle and upper Pleistocene, that fossils classed as members of the species *Homo sapiens* are first found. This means that the splenium too has been part of the human brain for at least one hundred millennia. Since the only known function it appears to serve depends upon there being written material for individuals to interpret, and writing is probably no older than 6,000 years, either the splenium existed without function for many thousands of years, or such functions are as yet unknown. In either case, its importance in reading is modern, and the importance of the splenium *to* reading is critical.

Our hypothesis is that in order for an individual to become literate, it is first essential that the connections in the neurological system serving reading be put to use. Moreover, we think that the evidence on the social functions of literacy (like that presented at the start of this essay) suggests that if this is to happen, reading and writing must be valued as tools for pursuing some other goal. But simply making the connection active may only help us to understand how people become functional readers. It is not unlikely that the passage from functional to proficient reading depends not simply upon making the splenium functionally useful in a rudimentary way, but on "exercising" the connection. This would be the expected result of the process of very much continued reading and requires a context where there is high motivation to read and a variety of written material to interact with. (A more formal and precise way of expressing this is that the activation of the connection provided by the splenium may be necessary but not sufficient for the development of proficient reading. We think it helpful to conceive of this situation as somewhat like that of a ballet dancer; it is necessary to learn the basic positions of ballet (*demipointe, pointe,* and the *port de bras,* for example) before a dancer can master the art, but that alone is not sufficient— practice and continual exposure to ballet are required to become proficient.)

The achievement of literacy cannot depend solely upon context, motivation, and opportunity to make us put the splenium to work. If it did, then many adult literacy programs could be expected to produce large numbers of proficient readers. In fact, as we observed earlier, adult literacy programs have been only marginally successful, producing mostly functional readers. Our guess is that the splenium must be put to work early in an individual's life if proficient reading ability is to develop. Again this would not be an unusual circumstance. Many structures, even some in the brain, like those serving expressive spoken language, appear to have *critical periods* in their development.[4] These are periods during which a latent structure can be put to use and begin to serve a particular function, sometimes effortlessly, but after which the acquisition of that function by the structure becomes difficult or even impossible.

Lest this seem overly abstract, consider spoken language. For years anthropologists and linguists have said that any normal human infant is capable of learning to speak any human language, especially if the language being learned is part of everyday experience. Yet we also know that after a point in early adolescence people find it difficult or impossible to produce accurately some of the sounds of languages other than their own. Many English-speakers, for example, find it difficult to learn to speak accurately tonal languages like Chinese, and nearly impossible to master the click languages of Africa. (Again, it may be helpful to think of the ballet dancer. Some of the basic ballet positions require movements which, if not first learned while the limbs are relatively young and flexible, become possible only with some awkwardness, or not at all. While such movements are not constrained by critical periods in a strict sense, the analogy is helpful here too.)

We suggest, then, that there is a critical period during which the neurological system serving reading must be put to work if proficient reading is to be developed. If this is so, it is important that we discover just when in the course of a child's development this period begins, and how long it lasts. Finding out if there is such a critical period for the activation of the splenium, and *if* there is, what are its onset and duration, form questions for empirical investigation. We think it likely that such investigation will show more clearly the role of the splenium, and of the right hemisphere, in reading, and we think it probable that some critical period for the development of that role will be found as well.

We expect that not only a critical period for the functional development of the splenium will be evidenced, but also that an identifiably critical role in achieving proficient reading will be found to be played by the splenium. The basis for this conjecture is what we know of VPA's experience. Due apparently to the disruption of the connection provided by the splenium, VPA ceased, literally in one stroke, to be a proficient reader. He lost an ability not that he was born with but that he once developed by personal effort when he was young enough to do so. Indeed, after two years of effort and practice VPA remains a functional reader; although he has developed in this time a number of strategies that minimize the errors he makes, the disruption of the splenium's functioning appears to mean that proficient reading will never again be possible for him.

If the process we have described is the case, we next may ask: If one does not develop proficient reading while a child, does this mean that one will never be able to develop this skill? On the basis of the above speculations we think the answer is likely to be "Yes," except perhaps in extraordinary cases, because the important interhemisphere connection provided by the splenium was never made functionally active. This connection appears only to be made when a person reads enough, and with enough speed and ease, to become nearly a proficient reader. This in turn suggests that, if widespread literacy is taken as an important goal, we must first be concerned that the connection gets to be functional, not particularly how refined this activity is. This means we must start people reading at an age early enough to fall within the presumed critical period. Our opinion is that we must design ways of creating settings in which children become relatively proficient readers before adolescence.

This description has some fairly direct consequences for the teaching of literacy skills to children. In colonial, postcolonial, and other plural societies, educators and social activists have long debated what the language of instruction in schools should be. Usually the argument centers on whether some indigenous language (say an English Creole or an Indian language) or some "cosmopolitan," "standard" language (like English or Spanish) should be the language used in the schools. Typically the debate's argument is carried out on a social level, proponents of each view pointing out the social motivations for, and the social benefits thought to derive from, teaching children in one of the languages. For example, in much of South America the conflict is between the use of a native Indian language, such as Quechua, and Spanish; in the United States the question often concerns the proper role, if any, of "Black English."

In general, we think that the social arguments against the casual requirement that the "standard" language be the exclusive language of instruction in schools are correct. Our interpretation of studies in comparative education is that when children (or, for that matter, adults) are put in the position of being forced to study in a language other than their own, and for which they feel little affinity, they find themselves torn between the different social identities that using the second language implies. The consequences of these kinds of situations also appear to us negative because, at a minimum, sound, meaning, and visual input must be brought together in familiar context if the functional utility for reading of the neurological system is to be established. (A Mayan-speaking child who sees the printed word "casa" may never recognize, unless coached in the proper setting, that it is the rough equivalent of "nah.")

Unless the sound/meaning relationship and the meaning/ written word relationships are clear to children, the neural pathway linking visual input to linguistic interpretation will not be established or reinforced. Wallace Lambert has defined these situations as "subtractive." His research shows that when the teaching of a language is intended to replace rather than supplement a child's first language, the consequences are feelings of pressure and a threatened and unstable sense of social or ethnic identity.

Our own research with children in Central America and the United States suggests that these subtractive situations also have negative psychological consequences. This, too, argues against the indiscriminate use of the notion that, because it will allow students to participate in the world community, teaching in a standard language is always the best educational practice. In fact, to the extent that it keeps children from establishing the functional utility of the splenium, by increasing stress and social insecurity and by reducing motivation to read, that practice may well keep children outside of the larger community.[5]

This point can and has been argued on the basis of social and psychological data. We here propose the addition of a physiological reason for preferring the view that educators should take as their first priority the teaching of children to read at an early age, even if it must be in a vernacular, nonstandard language. Indeed, if establishing the functional utility for reading of the portions of the brain used for reading is as critical as we think it is, then the case for starting children to read the earliest possible, regardless of the "correctness" of the language they first learn to read in, is considerably strengthened.

Teilhard understood life to be a process in which individuals interact with their environment to affect eventually the course of human evolution. In this context our discussion of literacy suggests that the process by which this happens requires, through teaching and individual effort, that we develop and use neurological potentials the functions of which are not genetically given, but which have the result of universalizing human culture and society, if only by permitting us to read.

Notes

1. For further discussion of this and related views of literacy, see J. Goody and I. Watt, "The Consequences of Literacy," *Comparative Studies in Society and History*, vol. 5, 1963; J. Goody, ed., *Literacy in Traditional Societies* (New York: Cambridge University Press, 1968); and, P. Freire, *Pedagogy of the Oppressed* (New York: Seabury Press, 1970).

2. For more information about Cherokee literacy and social organization, see Sol Tax and Robert Thomas, "Education 'For' American Indians: Threat or Promise?," *The Florida FL Reporter*, vol. 7, 1969; Albert Wahrhaftig, "The Tribal Cherokee Population of Eastern Oklahoma," *Current Anthropology*, vol. 9, 1968; and, John White, "On the Revival of Printing in the Cherokee Language," *Current Anthropology*, vol. 3, 1962.

3. Accessible general introductions to an understanding of the brain can be found in J. C. Eccles, *The Understanding of the Brain* (New York: McGraw-Hill, 1973; and M. G. Wittrock, ed., *The Human Brain* (Englewood Cliffs, NJ: Prentice-Hall, 1977). The most direct entrance to work on the alexias can be found in Norman Geschwind's work. Particularly accessible are his contributions, "Some Differences Between Human and Other Primate Brains," in *Cognitive Processes of Nonhuman Primates*, L. Harrard, ed. (Academic Press, 1979), and "The Development of the Brain and the Evolution of Language," *Monograph Series on Language and Linguistics*, No. 17, 1964.

4. For more on structure and function in evolution, see Stephen J. Gould, *The Panda's Thumb* (New York: Norton, 1980); Earl W. Count, *Being and Becoming Human: Essays on the Biogram* (New York: Van Nostrand, 1973); C. D. Laughlin, Jr. and E. G. d'Aquili, *Biogenetic Structuralism* (New York: Columbia University Press, 1974). The last discusses latent structures, critical periods, and the evolution of the human brain. Eric Lenneberg's *Biological Foundations of Language* (New York: Wiley, 1967), discusses critical periods in the acquistion of language.

5. The social and psychological consequences of subtractive language settings are discussed more fully in Wallace Lambert's paper, "Culture and Language as Factors in Learning and Education," in *Cul-*

tural Factors in Learning and Education, Aboud and Mead, eds. (Western Washington State College, 1974); R. A. Rubinstein, "The Cognitive Consequences of Bilingual Education in Northern Belize," *American Ethnologist,* vol. 6, 1979; and Sol Tax, "Self and Society," in *Reading in Education: A Broader View,* M. Douglass, ed. (Columbus, OH: Charles E. Merrill, 1973).

Part Two

MIND/SPIRIT

THE VISION IS THE REALITY

Elise Boulding

As a very small child I had a vivid sense of the connectedness of heaven and earth. It happened every Christmas eve as my mother and father took me by the hand and we walked sedately around the star-lighted Christmas tree in the darkened living room singing Norwegian carols. We sang about a little baby who was a great king but came down to earth every Christmas. The tree was lit for his coming. He always went back to his castle in heaven when Christmas was over, but I have a distinct image of Jesus the King, sitting by an open window in his castle in the heavens, listening to the prayers of children from earth in the long stretches of months between Christmases. The sky never felt distant, but near. Heaven was roomy and full of love. This made me feel very secure at night. I loved the dark because I could feel heaven. I could feel the stars, too, even when the night sky was overcast and they could not be seen.

I somehow grew up with the ability to feel the faraway as near. Because I could imagine that heavenly castle in my mind, I knew it was also *in me*. (The intuition that what they imagine outside them is also inside them often comes to very young children, about the age of three.) It was many years later before I understood the full meaning of "the kingdom of heaven is within," but the ground of that understanding came very early indeed. When I was eleven I read a story in the Sunday papers

I loved to look at on weekends. It was about how matter was mostly empty space with some molecules bouncing around in it and that delighted me. Then I knew that the earth beneath my feet was really the same substance as the starry sky above me—it just *seemed* more solid. This was such a splendid way of seeing that I told all my friends about it. The information which delighted me left them blank and disbelieving. I was disappointed that they could not see what was so obviously true. Years later, when I read a passage in an article about general systems describing a stone as a society of molecules moving about within a bounded space, I experienced the same delight I knew as a child. For me solid surfaces are diaphanous, and the real world I live in is one of dancing molecules. They dance under my feet, they dance in the sky, and they dance in my head and my heart. I cannot easily distinguish between an inward dance of the molecule and the inward dance of the spirit which I feel as prayer.

The discovery that a great scientist who was also a great Christian teacher and Jesuit priest experienced the world the same way I did was a very happy discovery. Teilhard de Chardin had the same absurd conviction as I that matter and apparently empty space and spirit were one and the same, that within was without and without was within. He also knew that something was working itself out in every corner of the cosmos, all appearances to the contrary notwithstanding. His childhood experience was different from mine, but I recognized it as another path to the same insights. Teilhard's account in *The Heart of Matter* of his childish adoration of the solidity of iron and of his collection of treasured iron objects, I found very moving, particularly as he had to experience the trauma of discovering that iron rusts. Out of his intense need to know what he could count on came his vision of the oneness of matter and spirit. My discovery was a much gentler, kinder experience.

We underestimate our early childhood inward journeys. We need to understand even better than we do how a young heart can fall in love with the universe, how a young mind can begin ordering the cosmos. We are all universe-lovers, I suspect, we who are writing the essays in this book. Teilhard certainly was. But there are not that many universe-lovers around today. We live in grim times, and much of the arts and letters, to say nothing of the sciences of these times, reflect that grimness. Where does Teilhard and those who with him are universe-lovers stand in relation to our time?

The Century Behind Us
I will use my favorite device of the two-hundred-year present to answer. If we think of 1981 as marking the midpoint of that two-hundred-year present, looking back one hundred years to Teilhard's birth in 1881 and forward one hundred years to 2081 when the babies born today may reach their hundredth birthday, it may help to clarify changing perceptions of reality. In 1881, nineteenth-century optimism that the deity could be pensioned off because science was going to solve the problems of war, poverty, and disease, and that "man" was going to be able to make a utopia of earth all on "his" own was at its height. The series of world fairs that began in 1850 in Paris made the world seem small, cozy, and manageable. (The specific realities of life on the vast continents of Africa, Asia, and Latin America and the nature of our colonizing activities there were conveniently blurred in people's minds.) International science, social welfare, and civic organizations were forming at a rapid rate, and the church had given up the eschatological vision of the millenium to settle for the social gospel here and now.

World War I shook that faith. The flaming wildness of the 1920s startled the serious-minded; the depression led to questioning about the skills of the social designers of utopia; World War II led to questions about the moral fiber of the European home of Western civilization; and Vietnam led to questioning the moral fiber of the United States, outpost of that civilization. In the post-Vietnam era the fruits of science and technology have come to be perceived by many as fraught with horror. Worldwide militarization and rising levels of violence; chemical pollution of soil and water and air, some from apparently harmless long-established local factories, some from increasingly dreaded nuclear plants; signals that some precious planetary resources including soil are being exhausted; and finally the increasing incapacity of governmental regulatory systems to control these fruits for the benefit of the citizenry have led to the most serious questioning of all: Can human beings use science and technology for the good of the social order? The utopian prophecies that still seemed plausible before World War I have nearly all disappeared, to be replaced by bleak scenarios of the fizzling out of the human race.

But Teilhard was born in 1881. Optimism was part of his shaping. He was nourished by roots that fed at deep underground springs, untouched by the spiritual drought of world wars, depression, technology run wild. Others also held to that earlier faith. Biologists Julian Huxley and Ludwig Bertalanffy saw a principle in biological processes that was order-creating in a profoundly spiritual sense. Historians Arnold Toynbee and H. G. Wells saw the same order-creating process in history. Fred Polak, born just after the turn of the century, saw the visioning itself as the order-creating process, and feared it was breaking down because he saw his own contemporaries losing their visioning capacity, retreating to the present moment. He saw himself as standing at a breach in history, and indeed the breach was real.

Perhaps 1920, the year I was born, was almost the last in which the old utopian spiritual formation was possible. My co-authors and readers who are sixty and older will recognize what I mean. Each shock of social evil sent our roots down deeper as we sought for the means to sustain our vision of the good. I have conducted interviews with individuals in a series of generational cohorts, beginning with those born in 1910 and ending with those born in 1950, and find that those born in 1910 and 1920 sustained great struggles with the problem of evil, but somehow retained a sense that life basically tended toward the good. Most of those born in 1930 and after grew up feeling that life was beset with dangers and evil, and that good might not prevail. Those who eventually mastered their despair sought and found sources of social and spiritual (though they might not call them spiritual) nourishment outside mainstream thought and action (cf. Boulding, "Evolutionary Visions," 1980).

The Century Ahead of Us

Teilhard died in 1955, but in a sense it is to the generation born in that decade that he was sent. He was an intellectual and spiritual friend and guide to those of his own generation who shared his proscopic capacity to look through the present to the future, but to the postwar generation he has been a teacher across the breach of time. He has been sending out the signals of the new age across the breach, and those young people who have been listening have caught the signals. Now we are entering the second half of this two-hundred-year present, and the effects of Teilhard's visioning grow stronger every day. If the Teilhard Foundation which is publishing this book did not already exist, it would certainly have to be invented now to respond to the growing demand to hear that there is an alternative to a nuclear holocaust for humankind.

While Teilhard's vision is time-transcending, he is also very much a product of that unique blend of scientific and religious optimism which obtained a century ago. His vision is indeed a time bomb in the Polakian sense of images of the future as time bombs (Polak, 1953), but one which will explode not in the next century or the one after, but only several centuries into the future when tribalism and nationalism have evolved toward more inclusive social identities rooted in a profounder sense of local identity. The social soil is not yet ready. In the meantime we should think of the coming century as the period in which we work out the evolutionary vision in the broader context than the Eurocentric, homocentric frame of Teilhard's thought.

His Eurocentrism was so strong that he was able to spend a large portion of his life in China without ever perceiving more in Eastern civilization than "passivity" (*The Phenomenon of Man*, p. 296). His homocentrism was so strong that he could only perceive the feminine principle as something that nourished males (*The Heart of Matter*, p. 58). In short, non-Western civilizations and women remained essentially outside the social order which he saw evolving at the heart of, and interpenetrating with, the cosmic order. The human race will not be ready for the rest of the vision until those kinks are straightened out. It will be a long, slow process and may take several centuries. But in straightening them out, we will create the conditions for the psychic evolution of the Human Million which Teilhard saw in a vision near Verdun in 1916.

By placing Teilhard in a cohort of evolutionary visioners toward the end of the last century, I do not mean to underplay the uniqueness of his vision. No thinker before Teilhard had caught the multiple interplay of forces in the mind-society-spirit relationship as he has done. No one else has been able to use the understanding of that interplay to recreate the history of the planet and to write the history of its end, staying within the bounds of scientific concepts. Finally, no one envisioned such a process as hominization/Christification of the planet, thus bringing a new dimension to the Christian vision. While scientists complain of his science and Christians complain of his theology, his vision is a unitive experience defying all explanations of the relationships between science and religion, and bearing its validity within itself.

By developing the concept of the noosphere, Teilhard taught us what kind of species humanity is. By pointing out that the organic potential of the whole of planetary evolution existed from the very beginning of earth's formation, he reminds us that there is planetary fulfillment ahead, and that we are responsible for developing every bit of potential that lies in our hands. Teilhard was one of the first to develop the concepts of general systems theory, so important to science in this century. It was he who insisted to a fractionated and fractionating scientific community that it must see wholes and live and work in the constant present of the Omega which is the Alpha, a metaphor for vastly greater time scales than science was accustomed to. More than all that, he loved every molecule of creation with a passion that transformed every scientific observation and every piece of metaphysical reasoning into an act of worship. Teilhard danced before the altar of the Lord, like

David. Finally, Teilhard will not let us stand outside and watch. We must be inside the great Christification process, because there is no without; all without is within.

Reconstructing the Vision

Every generation must work at the reconstruction of vision. As Polak said in *The Image of the Future,* we have no future except what we can envision, and what we can vision will draw us toward itself. In the reflections that follow, I suggest several areas of reconstruction of vision, building on Teilhard's work but bringing different perspectives to bear on the construction process.

Before the Noosphere

Teilhard thought of the barysphere (his beloved iron) as the core of the planet, with the lithosphere, hydrosphere, biosphere, and atmosphere a series of successive envelopes. With the emergence of the noosphere, the "envelope of thought," that aspect of the evolutionary process which Teilhard calls hominization or spiritualization of the planet begins. In this view, the interpenetration of the spheres begins only with thought.

From the perspective of the social scientist, the leap from the biosphere to the noosphere as a transformational envelope is too sudden and leaves out a whole stage in the complexification process that Teilhard otherwise describes so well. He points out, correctly, that the species *sapiens* already appears on the planet as a "crowd"; the long period of becoming human will probably always remain invisible to us. When we see humans, they are already in groups. (Of course, we might add, since their animal forebears and contemporaries also live in groups.) But the human group has distinctive properties, because in interaction humans are able to create mental representations of each other in a great variety of configurations, and out of that process of mental representation and the symbolic interaction associated with it, grows the social order or the sociosphere. (The term was first used, I believe, by Kenneth Boulding in *A Primer in Social Dynamics,* 1970.)

I suggest that we are now in another of those long evolutionary gestation periods comparable to the one which produced the species *sapiens,* and that what is being formed is even yet scarcely visible. Only, because we are sapient, can we name that which is emerging even in its incipient stages. This new phenomenon, the sociosphere, is the planetary web of social interactions (Teilhard would call it "skin" or "envelope"). The road from sapiens in groups to sapiens in a differentiated set of interacting units cooperating to maintain a world order is a very long one. Each set of links, economic, political, sociocultural, is being slowly and painfully formed. Currently we have a somewhat feeble international (meaning inter-nation) order, but we are a long way from a social order on a world scale. Since evolutionary action operates to differentiate units even while integrating them, concepts of world government, at least as they presently exist, do not take us in this direction. The United Nations and its agencies, other intergovernmental organizations, the world web of more than 4,000 international nongovernmental organizations, groupings of citizens across national boundaries based on shared interests, all represent fragments of an emerging sociosphere, continually suffering rents and tears through violence and war. In my interpretation of evolution, only when there is a relatively unviolent sociosphere will the differentiation-centration processes of human symbolic interaction be able to generate the planetary web of thought that Teilhard calls the noosphere.

The noosphere is incipient in the sociosphere, of course, just as the sociosphere is incipient in the biosphere. In fact, nothing happens in orderly stages, for the molecules of one phenomenal form continually interpenetrate other phenomenal forms, as Teilhard himself knew. His envelope metaphor gets in the way of an interpenetration metaphor. Between barysphere, lithosphere, hydrosphere, cryosphere (the frozen ice masses of the planet), atmosphere, stratosphere, sociosphere, and noosphere there is a continual slippage of particles, a slow molecular ballet. No longer can scientists of any one discipline work alone, because we have to know the interaction at the interfaces of each set of spheres (and each interfaces with every other) in order to understand any process at all in depth. The best example of this is the current effort to study global climate change. Since there has been no climatic equilibrium state for the planet in its long history, scientists would like to know whether the signals which seem to suggest a possible global climate warming with a melting of the ice caps are in fact pointing to such a process or whether they are pointing to the opposite—a global climate cooling and the onset of a historically recurring ice age. Because science cannot yet model the interaction of forces within and between each of these spheres, even at the nonbiological level, the question of what is happening to the climate cannot now be settled. When the interactions involving the biosphere and the sociosphere are added, the possibilities of answers recede into the rather distant future.

Yet we must act, take decisions, since human welfare is at stake. Because the noosphere is not yet developed and the sociosphere is very imperfectly connected, decisions taken by nation states to try to protect "their" peoples may well precipitate climate wars. The respective defense departments of the superpowers are already writing scenarios of what they fear their adversaries may do. Not only is our knowledge very partial, but our ability to think for the planet as a whole is almost nonexistent. Teilhard's conception of our present evolutionary stage slips our species a little too quickly into the role of conscious participant in evolution. Most of the time we really do not know what we are doing. It will be a long time before we even know who "we" are in a planetary sense, let alone understand the processes which we are affecting but hardly guiding. We may be the "leading shoot," but this does not really tell us very much about the process that is putting us there. We are not yet ready or able to have planetary intentions.

Evolution as a Transcivilizational Process
Teilhard not only sees the human species as the "leading shoot" of evolution, but he sees Western Christians as the tip of the leading shoot. To the extent that he mentions other civilizational traditions at all, he sees them either as inert obstacles to change or as forces of evil along with the uneradicated forces

of evil within the West. These forces *may* persist and continue to harass the evolutionary process, but will in the end be spun off into outer darkness in a cataclysmic process out of which the Christified/spiritualized planet will emerge. It is a bit startling to find this Zoroastrian theme (which lived on in Christianity also) emerging in Teilhard. He is not sure about this theme, but brings it up several times as a possibility.

A concept of evolution that does not include the evolution of the human capacity to choose the good is certainly thinkable, but is discordant with a recurring theme of all civilizational traditions, a vision embodying both the nurturant and the assertive traits of humanity.[1] If we look at the literature of Antiquity we find recurring images of human beings living peacefully together "in a garden." In this garden there is abundance, there is sharing, there is joy. The nomads of the Middle Eastern deserts, the Greeks who farmed the stony soil of Attica, and the Norse who farmed even stonier soil by the North Sea, all knew the image of the abundant and peaceful garden. Both nomads and settled folk had the image. Sometimes these images are of a golden age in the past, sometimes they represent visions of a coming age or an after-life. What is interesting is that they all have in common an idea of human togetherness and sharing; fighting to kill or take captive is eliminated from the scene. One might label these legends cultural potentials for peaceableness. They are in various ways reflected in the ideal social order of each imaging society, in its laws, and in its treaties with other nations after wars. The fact that such images come from well-known warrior societies makes them all the more interesting. It is noteworthy that these images are describing warriors who have become androgynous beings.

Teilhard's tendency to see other civilizations and their religious faiths as dead, fossilized entities instead of living traditions, still growing and developing alongside the Western civilization and its Christian tradition, limits his understanding of the evolutionary process on a planetary scale. It can be argued that it is particularly difficult for Westerners to develop a true planetary perspective because the West has been engaged in technological and military expansion and conquest for five hundred years. Conquerors know the terrains they have conquered only in the most superficial way. Because Western Christian thought is also profoundly hierarchical, it rules out understanding on nonhierarchical conceptions of evolution and development. Teilhard's thinking is strongly hierarchical. He speaks of "cephalization"—the development of the head—as a basic evolutionary process. The development of the head is what makes the human species human, and the human species in turn becomes the head of evolution on the planet.

All civilizational traditions have concepts of hierarchy, since this represents a useful device for an administrative center to relate in an orderly manner to a large number of interacting units. Its development throughout history (and each civilization has insights about the nature and danger of hierarchy) has been pragmatic. Only the West has elevated hierarchy into an ultimate moral principle. Islam, Buddhism, and Hinduism are all profoundly antihierarchical at the same time that they hold a clear vision of *development*. Taoism provides an interesting example of an antihierarchical vision of development.

Taoists were committed to the observation of nature rather than the management of society. Joseph Needham finds a profoundly scientific mentality among them. Nature taught them processes of change and development that involved no external application of force. The action of water has a favorite process metaphor:

> What is of all things most yielding
> Can overwhelm that which is most hard,
> Being substanceless it can enter in even where there is no crevice.
> That is how I know the value of action which is actionless.
> But that there can be teaching without words,
> Value in action which is actionless
> Few indeed can understand.
> (chap. 43, *Tao Te Ching*, quoted in Needham, 1962, vol. 2, p. 57)

The prescriptions for social policy which Taoists drew from their observations of nature were essentially localist and minimally governmental. The yin-yang theory that emerged from the Chinese study of nature can be interpreted as a theory of dissipative systems.[2] The yin and yang, or the polarities of light and dark, dry and wet, firm and yielding, are continuously interpenetrating one another and obliterating all boundaries and form, conceptual and physical, yet new boundaries and forms continually emerge from the process. For the Taoist it is the process that counts. Reality is in a continual state of emergence. By intuiting and following along with the process, humans can bring the social order into alignment with the Tao, the cosmic order. According to Needham, there are clear evidences of evolutionary concepts associated with Taoism, particularly related to the development of biological forms (cf. Needham, 1962, vol. 2, pp. 78–80; in Boulding, "Evolutionary Visions," 1981).

One of the early modern statements of Hindu development thinking is found in Gandhi's concepts of *sarvodaya*, the welfare of all, of *aparigraha*, not wanting what others can't have, and *satyagraha*, a process of becoming through nonviolent action. The becoming, the betterment of the human condition, takes place in community and the welfare of the individual and of the community are inseparable. The concept of *sarvodaya* has been independently redeveloped in Sri Lanka by A. T. Ariyaratna in the *Shramadana* movement, which links spiritual awakening at all levels from the individual to the planet, with a concept of giving of the awakened energy in service to others.[3]

Developmental concepts in Islam are based on the Tauhid, a "worldview in which the universe is regarded as a unity, with a single form, possessing will, intelligence, and purpose that is God" (Albert, *Tell the American People, 1980*, p. 157. There is no private ownership in the Tauhid, only stewardship of the earth's resources which are to be equally shared by the community. The Islamic conception of the interpenetration of the sacred and the secular has been rejected in the West, which sees the world in terms of a sacred-secular dichotomy with secularization as the prevailing trend. Teilhard, whose evolutionary concept of divinization is very much in harmony with Islamic conceptions, apparently did not see the potential in this remarkable post-Christian, anticlerical, strongly egalitarian community of faith whose adherents number close to one-seventh of humankind and who call themselves the people of the Book. In so doing they acknowledge their kinship with other "peoples of the Book," Jews and Christians. During Europe's Dark Ages, Islam was the "leading shoot of evolution," bursting forth from the lands bordering the Mediterranean. We are forcibly reminded today of the dynamics which remains in this world view. It is difficult to discern evolutionary direction in the midst of contemporary war and violence, but we should note that some Moslems are speaking of the need to move out of the darkness and backwardness of the West—what they call "Westoxication"—and into the light. This is strange language to Christian ears and must be pondered carefully.

This is a transition time and we must look well to see where new growth is springing forth. A very reasonable hypothesis would be that each civilizational tradition, each community of faith, is bringing forth its own new shoots, and that God makes use of each for planetary processes very imperfectly understood by any one of the communities. Not one of these faiths is stranger to the mystical unitive experience, to the tension of expectant waiting, to the knowledge of the arrow of longing that pierces the Cloud of Unknowing. The gifts that each religion continually offers the human spirit are a longing for oneness with creation, and for goodness.

Teilhard's vision of hominization underestimates the goodness problem. His delight and joy in his work as a scientist and his delight and joy in the presence of God, led him to overleap a vast terrain the human collectivity must yet traverse. It is because Teilhard overestimated science and human mentation that he underestimated the goodness problem. He did not foresee the extent to which scientific knowledge would be used for weapons of destruction, and how difficult it would be to channel the fruits of life-giving scientific research to the poor. The West gets more than its share of blame for failures to share the benefits of science and technology with the poor at home and abroad. The moral consciousness of the human species long ago evolved to the point of understanding the ethic of sharing; the universality of the images of the peaceable garden with its shared abundance in all cultures tells us that. The harnessing of that moral consciousness to intention and will and skill has yet to take place in any religious faith or cultural tradition. The evolutionary potential of the vision of sharing lies in its capacity to draw all communities toward its realization, but the process will be a long one.

Evolution as a Trans-Gender Process

The work of civilization has been perceived as the work of men. Women have historically stood outside the social order, bearing a special responsibility for its reproduction and maintenance. Valued as mothers and nurturers of the species, and symbolically as the Mother of God, women have not been perceived as formulators, shapers, and co-participants in the social order either in its religious or civic dimensions. The falsity of this ascription of biological purpose to women and civic purpose to men was perceived long ago by Plato. In *The Republic* he visualizes both women and men being trained as guardians in his ideal society since both genders have, he points out, the same capacities. He backed off in *The Laws*, however, for the reason that men through the centuries have backed off from the recurring insight that the capacities of the species are distributed equally between the genders: men have been socialized to dependency on women and to personal helplessness to such an extent that they are insecure and fearful, unable to imagine a society where they are not "cared for," where nurturance is a mutual task between women and men. Their exclusion from parenting and the ignominious competition with their own children for attention from the wife-mother reenforce their already deep-seated conviction that they *need* nurturance, but cannot *give* it.[4]

Teilhard is, of course, heir to this traditional view. He writes, "I have experienced no form of self-development without some feminine eye turned on me, some feminine influence at work" (*The Heart of Matter*, p. 59). In his view of the evolutionary process, the work of centration/hominization/divinization is done by men who are watched over by women. While the men become ever-more-differentiated beings, the women remain the same. A transformation process accomplished by half the human species under the watchful eye of the other half is a manifest absurdity. One of the major preconditions for evolutionary development in the social order is the development in men of their atrophied nurturance capacities and the development in women of their atrophied civic capacities. There has, of course, always been "underground" nurturance on the part of men, both in their families and in their all-male groups (the well-publicized phenomenon of "male bonding"), just as there has always been "underground" civic work on the part of women. I have described the ways in which women shape the social order from below in *The Underside of History*. The lack of social legitimation of these underground activities for each gender persistently sours the good they do, and leads to mutual distrust and "the battle of the sexes."

An even more persistent and troubling aspect of the false division of labor between the sexes is the blurring of distinction between highly evolved spirituality and emotional insincerity in the behavior of women, and the blurring of distinctions between creative institution-building and conquest and dominance behavior in men. The separation of functions makes a travesty of the best in each. Full partnership between women and men in all spheres of human activity, with individual personality bent and talent, rather than gender, determining particular roles, has to be the next item on the evolutionary agenda.

Evolution and the Childhood of the Species
Rereading Teilhard's very moving account of his own early intellectual-spiritual development in *The Heart of Matter*, and reliving my own childhood, I remembered for the thousandth time that children begin the work of constructing the universe very early. They are co-creators with God from birth, but most of their work of interior reflection and insight, their visioning and their prayer life, go on well hidden from the adult world.

Also the creative free-flowingness of those constructions gradually declines as children learn to put their untidy thoughts into the tidy boxes that adults, as parents and teachers, give them. We teach children the names of things, and take from them their own gift of naming. While few are born with the intellectual endowments of a Teilhard de Chardin, all are born with a gift for naming. All out-of-doors was Teilhard's classroom as a child, but most children only know indoor classrooms. Learning took place on family walks, giving life and meaning to what was learned sitting at a desk. Making unlikely connections between concepts and observations was Teilhard's everyday mental habit, but most children are punished for making unlikely connections. "No, no, it's not *that* way; it's *this* way!" This is as true during music and drawing and gym as during the teaching of the three R's. Who provides for the inward dance of the spirit for today's children of the average public school?

If we are to prepare for transformation we must begin moving children out of classrooms more of the time, and into a variety of community settings where every child's gift for making fresh and new connections will have free play. They will learn to see wholes because they will discover that their community is a living system. Biology, chemistry, geology, and physics need to be learned by ponds, rivers, fields, hills, and valleys, at the living interfaces between community and environment. Social and economic and craft skills and an understanding of human needs come best in the learning sites of repair shops, stores, production centers, farms, service and civic enterprises, and churches where adults and children are teacher-learners and learner-teachers across all the ages of the life span, and no one stands outside. Spiritual growth comes best in solitary places, though true solitude is the last thing we offer children. Loneliness we offer, but not solitude. How can we carry out their personal/planetary transformational tasks?

The evolutionary task of transformation is staggering to conceive at any stage in the planet's history, but most difficult for our own times. The learning tasks are numerous beyond counting and the speeded-up process of complexification, as we experience it, taxes the adult mind and spirit to the utmost. In one sense, our children begin ahead of us, because they accept as part of their environment complexities we had painfully to master. We separate children too soon from their own community complexities, wanting to prepare them for tomorrow in the way we were prepared for today. Resisting the concept of progressive differentiation of the mental life of the species through the generations, we want to place our children in our mold, and use the classroom as the tool for accomplishing this. We must redefine the educational task and the educational process. Teilhard has taught us, as can our own memories, that children begin knowing the within and the without of life very early. If we give them the amplitude of opportunities that Teilhard had, to be anchored experientially in the realities of local complexity, they will know better then we imagine, how to grasp complexities of a greater scale. They will be able to make planetary connections we cannot now visualize. We are not ready for the transformation, but they may be.

As the Brothers of Weston Priory have been singing at Vigils the weekend this essay has been written in their guest house:

> We go on waiting, knowing you have come
> Yet we are not ready to be transformed.
> Give us your Spirit and we'll carry on.
> The day is long ahead of us and we'll carry on,
> And we'll carry on.
>
> *Weston Priory, Vermont*
> *10-27-80*

Notes

1. See, for example, the following: Macpherson, *Four Stages of Man*, p. 123; Thomas Bullfinch, *Bullfinch's Mythology* (New York: Crowell, 1947), p. 271; Peter Andreas Munch, *Norse Mythology: Legends of Gods and Heroes*, trans. by Sigurd Bernhard Bustvedt, revised by Magnus Olsen (New York: American Scandinavian Foundation, 1926), p. 48; Micah 5; Revelations 22:1-2; Koran 76 in W. Montgomery Watt, *What Is Islam?* (New York: Praeger, 1968), pp. 11-12; and for images of peace in statecraft, see: UNESCO, *Birthright of Man*, pp. 27, 31-32, 98, 115, 403, 465, 554.

2. The theory of dissipative systems is an evolutionary theory of development and change associated with the work of Ilya Prigogine. It postulates that new order, new equilibria will occur at the points of maximum disorder in an existing system.

3. As far as I know nothing is available about this movement in English now, but a book is in preparation by Joanna Macy.

4. For further elaboration of these ideas, see Susan Moller Okin, *Women in Western Political Thought* (Princeton University Press, 1979), and Dorothy Dinnerstein, *The Mermaid and the Minotaur* (New York: Harper & Row, 1976).

Other Works Referred to in the Text

Albert, David H. *Tell the American People, Perspectives on the Iranian Revolution.* Philadelphia: Movement for a New Society, 1980.

Boulding, Elise. *The Underside of History.* Boulder: Westview Press, 1976.

———. "Evolutionary Visions, Sociology and the Human Life Span." In *Evolutionary Visions,* edited by Eric Jantsch. Boulder: Westview Press, 1980.

Boulding, Kenneth. *A Primer in Social Dynamics.* New York: Free Press, 1970.

Needham, Joseph. *History of Scientific Thought. Science and Civilization in China,* vol. 2. New York: Cambridge University Press, 1956.

Polak, Fred. *The Image of the Future (De Toekomst is Verleden Tyd),* tr. Elise Boulding, New York: Oceana Press, 1961. Abridged by Elise Boulding. San Francisco; Elsevier, 1972.

LOVE'S CONSPIRATORS: BUILDERS OF EARTH-HOUSE-HOLD

Francis Tiso

"Who are you, Buster?"

The most radical ideas are the most organic, the most centered on the earth and earth-processes. For Teilhard, the evolutionary principle conditioned his thinking to such an extent that rather than giving in to a sort of pessimistic determinism, he came to find hope in the very rawness of the biological processes that thrilled his imagination. His biological sense and his Christian, historical sensibility enabled him both to believe and to assert: The situation has changed. Humanity differs; now is not the past. Teilhard's opus brings to realization the words of Isaiah: "Remember ye not the former things, neither consider the things of old. Behold, I will do a new thing; now it shall spring forth." (Isaiah 43:18–19) The old spiritualities now yield, gradually, like the old forms in moist clay yield to the potter's hand as he shapes the clay into freedom, formlessness, and renewed form. New spiritualities must emerge, built upon an entirely new experience, a new level of hominization on this curved matrix, Earth.

The past is dead, in the sense that the high achievements of the ancient spiritualities, East and West, have carried us thus far but are no longer specifically applicable to our situation. Tibet has fallen; mystery has fled Catholicism; science has fed scripture into the paper shredder. At best, for a very few, ancient thought sketches in the map we may follow. And only a few great ones remain among us to teach, guide, and form the new ways with the broken Siegfried sword of power and heart. We need today a "tantra" that is truly universal and which draws upon the universal continuity (tantra-continuum) of energies to which all the wisdoms have alerted us. The noosphere itself begs for a tantra, a disciplined practice which will recognize the enormous latent energies of psyche that are seething in the dispersed foci of planetization. In a sense, we have now to take the step beyond the Bodhisattva vow by admitting that to forgo nirvana for the benefit of all sentient beings is not some sort of ultimate act of compassion (though it is certainly something of that); rather, it states the simple fact that our destiny is here in the ever-more-energized transformation of matter by spirit, spirit in matter, spirit in the world, earth recognized as one whole, one tantra, one continuum with heaven. There is neither nirvana nor heaven apart from our interrelatedness to all that is, and above all to persons.

We must also pass beyond a merely secular vision of reality. True, the secularization phenomenon cuts through our idolatries and superstitions; it recognizes the untenable dualisms of past mysticisms, ancient residues, dim cosmogonies that would pretend to diminish our anxieties about the universe. These fatal imaginings no longer have a hold on us; the desperate clinging to extrinsic morals and literalistic scriptural interpretation represent their final death rattle. The myths are no longer sung in sacred form to the youth of the tribe; there is no longer any tribe. We are electronically made one, and we reel backward in a terror that recognizes nothing. Stripped of the vision of *illo tempore*, of primordial and original acts that can only be replicated by the priestly caste, we are forced to confront the obvious, the immediate, the utterly real: this present moment is all we have, ever; the complete channel for reality is here and now, even on this page, and in the breath you draw as you read these lines. If we are not now honest with each other, when shall we be? If we do not now press onward with the hominizing energies of love, the intensity that gives moment-by-moment birth to personhood, when shall we do it? Where else but in this very moment of passage, from breath to breath, from line to line, from my mind to yours, is there any grace, any beatitude? Be here. Now.

Our striving to find others in the present who can hear us in our cries for help and our longing for love, in our hopes for enduring occasions of deep sharing, in creating environments conducive to the discovery and celebration of deep feelings—all these are the signs of noogenesis among us. Making clear the needs, wants, and discriminations that arise from our innermost identity sets in motion the personalizing energies that advance the labor of earth-building, of house-hold making, of noogenesis. Setting aside the residues of stale thought and manipulations liberates us for the task of engendering authentic love. It is difficult to imagine love without this clarity, this distinctness arising from the lively expression of the inner self. Indeed, in a similar way, it is difficult to imagine a genuine ethics without liberation from the assumptions and habits of the "superego"—that which St. Paul called "the law."

We resist at every step this path of humiliations and reversals; the intellect sets its minefields and throws up barricades. The passions and desires come disguised as needs and feelings. Compulsions masquerade as compassion and selflessness. The entire person is stretched and twisted by the neurotic manifestations of an inward *psychomachia;* the true self seems doomed to extinction in a yearning for loss and forgetfulness. At such a time, happy is the one who falls into the hands of a guide who tells the truth in love. Even more crucial than the guide, though, is the readiness of the one who seeks to be the true self to experience the contradictions and humiliations as power. Caught in the turmoil of a questioning heart in which doubt and faith contend in deadly combat, self-consciousness is ground to dust. There is a feeling: "I hardly know if I exist anymore." At first, a sort of terror, a sense of dread and aloneness. Then, very gradually, through what seems an ocean of pain, one is cast up on the uncertain but solid reef of a nameless freedom. One dares not speak too much of it.

In this long sea-journey, two of the great guides for us have been Thomas Merton and Pierre Teilhard de Chardin. In the great grace-mystery of love, they are sacraments. And in the way of sacraments and symbols, they present two sides of the one essential reality. They speak of the fact that humanity is unknown apart from the whole of the human race; that there is a social dimension to the solitary leap into the mystical heart of reality. Their lives signify that the energies of planetization depend on the broad dissemination of knowledge, on the nurturing of imagination, on the cultivation of radical liberty. This "tantra" or "practice" is completed and balanced by the careful nurturing of the inner person as receptacle for universal forces, as the locus wherein possibility (the product of the intellect) can be embodied in life. Hence, for Merton, the path to the future, toward the new tantra, demanded that he enter deeply into the ancient ways—the ways of the Fathers, of the monastic theologians, of the Zen masters, and of the primitive seen as primordial. He was, on one level, a sign of interiorization and tradition clearly recognized and authentically lived in the direction of global consciousness. Thus, he revitalized pathways that would otherwise have seemed dim and moribund. Yet Merton was also a great leaper, because in his hunt among traditions, he committed himself, his own flesh and blood, to the chase. Like Acteon, he glimpsed the love-goddess naked, he endured her allure as she bathed in the waters of transfigured consciousness, and, himself transformed by the wonder of what he saw (both wrathful and enticing), he was devoured by his own dogs . . . an enigmatic victim of faulty techology. Yet he died as one who both loved and despised the ways of cities; he was both hermit and movie freak, the contemplative who rode the subway.

Teilhard is the sign of mind enamoured of possibility, the visionary of the vast scale of becoming on our planet. He stands in contrast to Merton as the mystic of the trenches, of science, of technique, even of the atomic bomb. He is the electronic shaman, ever on the move, ever finding himself outside (ecstasis) himself in the labor of research. He was an unwilling exile to the deserts of Asia, for decades cut off from the intellectual and cultural foci that he felt to be the true wellsprings of the future of humanity. Yet, from his exile, he gained a perspective of such daring on those very centers of planetization that it was as if he had been the first space traveler, the first to risk a leap into the spirit-walk of the earth, seen by humans only ten years ago to rise in the sky over the moon in the astronauts' photograph "Earthrise." Teilhard was perhaps the first technological mystic; the first to be transformed by the laboratory into an enlightened being. Here was a man awed by humanity's lurch forward into self-consciousness in this most violent of centuries.

In our present situation, these two, the exile and the hermit, stand as revelatory lamps on their stands. An immense uncertainty hovers darkly over the nations of the world at this start of a new decade. Lacking leadership, fearful over the consequences of dwindling fossil energy, distressed over the day-to-day assaults that reflect the loss of social values, the inhabitants of our great cities enter a vast interior desert of dread, wondering if their daily toil creates nought but a vaster target for a foreign bomb. The city's psyche has become wilderness and the person is as one lost and isolated in a waterless valley. A time and place for Elijah, perhaps, but no Elijah appears.

The generalized cultural discouragement that began in the paroxism of the First World War has captured the citadels of America at last. And, like Europeans of fifty or sixty years ago, we are tempted to seek solace in various fascisms, various totalized world views, or else to cling to the Weimar glamor of uncritical liberalism. A few dreamers and visionaries propose solutions, create networks, publish stray books, appear on TV. Depending on the ego needs of the particular zoo in which they are displayed, the fantasies are great or small, stern or soft-edged with velour. Groups are formed, rules imposed, feelings probed, manifestos composed. Individuals undergo "processes" by which they hope to be transformed, by sitting, chanting, eating, expressing, repressing, breathing, getting enemas, indulging, relaxing, psychobabbling, or getting high. One hears of a spiritual supermarket, and winces at the fluorescent glare. The degree of risk undertaken is directly dependent on the hunger one brings to the bazaar. The hungers, including the ones we have known, are great, gnawing, and frequent.

The deep inner hunger and impoverishment that is felt by individuals is intensified by the more nebulous sense of a loss of intention, a forgetting of purpose, and even a forgetting of what one wants, much less of who one is. The atavistic response of the crowds to the U.S. hockey victory at the 1980 Winter Olympics reminds us of our need to accept even counterfeits of the sense of collective meaning and purpose. If only we could sharpen our vision so as to see the wide gaps between meaningfulness and meaning and between meaning and purpose. If my own question (the question that the Zen masters describe, that burns my guts like a red-hot ball of iron) is the question "Who are you, anyway, buster?" and I set it among those three words, I cannot help but find myself in three looking-glass universes, each of which negates the case-hardened steeliness of the laws of the other two.

Instead, my thoughts wander toward specks of light, like cool distant stars, that suggest an inner harmony within a moving cosmic wholeness. I practice contemplation, looking for constellations here below, on the muddy skin of Mother Earth.

The remembrance of vision and hope, held by one utterly suppressed in his lifetime, comes to me. I think of Teilhard as the grain of wheat, buried in a church preoccupied with thoughts barely remembered, germinating a vision of the real and the possible that sweeps away church, world, believer, and unbeliever in a torrent of hope. I remember my meditations on evolution in which his awesome genius showed the scope of all things in the sight of the Utterly Real; at those times, I spoke in homage to all the animals and all the plants and to the Earth herself in new words, and was filled with the healing power of all creatures. I joined Teilhard in his distant place, his mountaintop, and though I felt the cool breeze, I also knew the nearness of passion in that place. Teilhard is one whose incandescence is not diminished by remote perspective. I am, with him, in the obscure personal place of the Cross and Resurrection, and the lasting energy of love. With him, I am where the action is, and the contradiction that makes for soul- and earth-building.

Teilhard carries me into that utterly free Breath of the Divine Spirit, that ultimate freedom that accounts for matter and form, and emptiness; I let that freedom unfold in my love and passion, and it is all collected and at every moment offered back to me, if I am daring enough to welcome it back, to pour it out again into the primal mystery of being itself.

Every thing depends on every other one; all are of one freedom (not of one *substance,* but one liberty, one in openness to being) and one root-meaning. One heart. All are consciousness seeking to rise, to be fully awake and fully alive. In the presence of humanity, all that can be spoken is awe, for here evolving knows itself as evolving. It knows its choices and places tool-making hands around fate. That-which-is acquires a reflexive brain and hands. Some have worried about the self-improvement impulse, which is apparently reconciled with the Teilhardian vision. Yet I wonder if the compelling need to be in control, to be "good" and "well" rests comfortably for long with a metaphysics rooted in freedom and in the energies of the Earth. Freedom does not mean that we have the option to choose the nice over the nasty; freedom is a matter of heart-rending communion with radical truth.

What next? Must I be forever pushed by reflexivity outward, ever more subject to entropy, the eventual winding down of our energies toward infinite dispersion and absolute zero? All the explosive power of the arms race, all the walls and barriers of mind and group lead us there into the cold inner circle of Hell, where there is no motion, only crisp separateness. Teilhard proposed that not only at this late moment, but all along, there has been an energy that activates us, that turns us back from the headlong dive into the freezing abyss. The crystal state, he observed, is a dead end in evolving. But the randomness of the protein, so fragile and delicately wrapped and folded, so easily denatured, points more securely toward consciousness than does the dome of rock salt or the isolated splendor of diamond.

So, too, the randomness of the folds and furrows of the human surface of the planet, the noosphere (which means so much more than a sphere of *mind, nous*), even the violence of human structures, points securely to a great leap in consciousness and a very great liberation. We are led to look for these fragile accumulations of energy, form, and freedom, in the hope of glimpsing the Grail, the Philosopher's Stone, the presence of realistic hope in this present moment of ordinary reality. Teilhard takes us to the Grail Castle and lets us find our way toward that love which is the activation of energy and the goal of evolving, and which moves us with the same unmistakable touch as it moves the sun and the other stars.

But our hearts, having accepted the mysterious power in the present moment, long all the more for the "how": "What are we to do henceforth?" How to act? For if I mean to say any one thing, it is that there is no self-realization since there is no "self" to realize. There is no somewhere toward which we are going, though it is often poignant to speak that way. In truth, there is *now* alone, and that which occurs in the now is the only given and consistent context for illumination and liberation.

To the extent that we are surprised by what happens in the now, so much the better for us, if we can flex with it, if we can dance with all the forces merrily, both the wrathful and the compassionate energies. Not everyone, however, is a born dancer. This is where it matters very much that we make an environment that does not crush these little ones, but rather teaches us the steps and hints at the surprises, twists, and jumps that come along. In spite of the spiritual supermarket, there are no how-to books in the spiritual life. There is only an environment, a situation, and the possibility of freedom. Even our private, preverbal confusion is part of the possibility and the environment, perhaps even the most potent part. This tantra of which I have spoken is a tantra of confusion, of collage, of information overkill. It sorts nothing out, has no credentials and makes no claims. Hence it lives and is holy. Perhaps then, we may dare to speak, not of how-to-do-it but of incarnation, of making the idea fact, and thus of reverence for the moment in which we find ourselves, and in which we are truly found.

"Think globally; act locally."

Human beings are overwhelmed by the scope of world needs at the present time. The explosion of information has produced in many persons a kind of despair. Thus, the potential for world transformation that at first seemed so accessible through technology, through the increase in population, through the expansion of economies and the availability of data, is checked in its development by a reaction against knowledge and even against intellect itself.

The individual person only emerges in the context of the whole of humanity, with those most proximate providing the most intense formational influence. Teilhard himself affirmed the utter dependence of the person on the collectivity in the process of becoming.

The apparent alienation of the person (and of the mind from the heart) is in fact a collective issue, a political issue. It has to do with how people live with other people and influence one another. On one level, alienation is a problem of motivation and of the recognition of common goals. However, it may also be expressed in terms of the isolation of the individual in search of a sense of "self," and must be traced to its social and economic context for complete analysis. Indeed, the very refusal of individuals to acknowledge their complicity in political and economic systems contributes to their sense of alienation.

The political notion of "solidarity," on the other hand, is an attempt to combat alienation collectively. In the best sense, during a time of crisis, a sense of solidarity increases the psychic pressure on the whole "mass," provoking more frequent and intense interpersonal contacts and leading to deeper social awareness. In a revolutionary setting, these conditions may even evoke ever greater and freer acts of self-sacrifice and love. Although rarely seen, and hardly ever carried to completion, it is in political action that the tension between mind and heart, intellect and will, produces its most powerful and creative results among persons. Whether we examine the Cistercian reform of Benedictinism in the twelfth century or the impact of the French Revolution of 1789 on the intellectual and cultural history of Europe, or even so brief an historical moment as the movement against the war in Vietnam, 1966–73, we have ample evidence for the transformation of human consciousness by these mass movements. Political action is the beginning of a sense of history, but our human potential for political action needs to be scaled up from its present timidity and discouragement.

A possible way to scale up human potential toward effectiveness in confronting and solving worldwide problems is to set persons to work on *winnable* struggles, as the experience of the peace movement, civil rights movements, and grass-roots organizing has taught us. When persons learn how to organize, interact, and win on a small scale, their energies are released and expanded. Speaking politically, small wins train us for the larger struggles and give us experience that can be applied to larger issues.

This is by no means meant to negate the necessity for isolated symbolic acts of resistance. These acts of public witnesss emerge out of a very special context and serve as a prophetic watchdog on the dark forces of society. If ever there was need to speak of a "special vocation" it is here; the small, embattled communities that witness in this way know what I mean. My concern here, however, is that we not restrict political action only to the gestures of witness and resistance. Smashing the Beast, growing to spiritual maturity, seeking vision in ordinary reality, and learning to dance with the Cosmic surprise are not discretely placed tents in the religious sideshow. Someone has to speak to the folks who think they are the main event. The very processes by which one engages in this exchange have been labeled corrupt and corrupting by many in the various resistance movements. Yet I question how realistic that labeling can be, given the fact of human interdependence, which includes everyone in the human adventure and makes it impossible to deny that deep within me there is both a Shangri-La and an Auschwitz.

Even as we seek ways of dialogue with the Powers and the Beast, however, a very real danger would be to set up the goal of directly resolving the world's problems. Resolution of macrocrises of the scale of the population explosion, the food situation, the ecological time-bomb, the arms race, etc., can only be effected by widely dispersed efforts that may only be related analogically to these huge problems. Human minds at the present stage of evolution simply cannot conceive of solutions to global crises. Therefore, local action on a relatively small scale is the indispensable lever in disseminating the core of values that will create world community. Only on the local level, in concrete exemplifications (often embodied in small communities), are world-values credible and accessible to the majority of persons. The local level is also the training ground for minds that will go on to larger issues and more broadly activated solutions. The solution to vast human problems is located in rather modest milieux—precisely those milieux that enable us, "the little ones," to grow up in an environment that opens us to the freedom of which we have just spoken.

An additional aspect of the numbing effect of global problematics is the resurgence of eschatological or apocalyptic consciousness. There is much curiosity about ancient prophecies about the end of the world at this time in the public awareness. In some cases, the hope for a cataclysm, always followed of course by a Golden Age, is so extravagant that it can only be matched by the despair we feel when we contemplate the factual consequences of nuclear disaster on the earth. Where will be the "new age" when all biological life, if not utterly obliterated, is mutated beyond all possibility of recovery? Certainly a postthermonuclear world could not support human life. Theologians have termed such an enormity a moral evil comparable only to the crucifixion, i.e., deicide. The very term "morality" seems hardly capable of pointing to that which is at stake here.

The sustaining of human hope in the face of universal nuclear threat seems to require faith in the transformation of the human person in and through contact with a transcendant Reality. The personal and transcendant Ultimate One, confronting all Being and at the same time perfusing all Being, has been sought with love by the great mystics of all traditions, and also by the ordinary folk who have followed the way of human love, procreation, and honest labor, and whose hopes were sustained and whose hearts were transformed in their communion beyond verbalization with this Loving One.

Christianity, for example, in teaching of God Incarnate in Jesus, can both present the model of this kind of faith and hope and also delineate the characteristics of this model in terms directly applicable to the release of human energy. God's own *energia,* his *dynamis* (power), his grace, is available to all and is active among all persons in building the kingdom of God. The "kingdom" is ultimately a oneness, the single and harmonious extension of divine power throughout all that is. But the kingdom is experienced as dual-natured. As with any powerful symbol, its message is ambivalent: the kingdom is not of this world, yet it is within you. It is already here below, yet it comes from above. It has come already, yet in some sense it is yet to arrive fully. It is utterly spiritual (there they neither marry nor give in marriage), yet it is never divorced from matter. It is so irrevocably united with the destiny of the material creation that the eternal sacrament of the kingdom is the one Person, Jesus Christ, called by faith both true God and true man. In words full of awe and daring, the church claims that Ultimate Reality has definitively identified and united with humanity.

That Person, that singular instance of Humanity, chose and still chooses to identify himself with the "little ones"—the poor, the broken, the oppressed, the dispossessed, the outcast. In the experience of conversion, of "coming to oneself" in the midst of a life that would otherwise be self-centered, self-directed, and, in the end, self-destructive, the broken human person discovers the mystery of the kingdom: that the extension of divine power penetrates into the human milieu at its breaking points. Grace not only seizes upon and builds up nature, grace also bursts forth in the desert, in the dark, in chaos, in vulnerability, silence, and aloneness, and in abandonment. Yes, even in our "mistakes" and in painful, irreparable breakages, there is a portal of grace. And sin, as the *Exultet* proclaims at the Easter Vigil, may turn out to be a "happy fault." Such is the way by which God calls all our planning and controlling into question; all the "ways" and how-tos are relativized. This is also how we, who might convert the Beast or smash the Powers, are warned. First we must know and love our own brokenness and beastliness; through the rock-ledge faults of our character and through the dance of the power-beast we become shamans and channels for divine power that heals the nations.

In the writings of Chuang-Tzu, *Inner Chapters,* we see the same spiritual dynamism in the dialogue between Confucius and his student, Yen Hui. Yen Hui is full of plans, ideas and preconceived solutions that he plans to use on the violent Prince of Weh to convert him to right conduct. But it is perfectly evident to Confucius that Yen Hui has not realized the purity of Tao within, and his arrogance will be only too obvious to the Prince, whose wickedness will only increase under the influence of the half-baked sage. Only after Yen Hui is broken under the intense questioning of the Master, even to the point of doubting his own personal identity ("Who are you, anyway, buster?"), does he open up to the reality of Tao, the way of power that wells up into consciousness in the human only to the extent that the human person is open to the deep and counterpoised energies of nature itself. That is, the mystery of eternal change, of dying and rising. In Christianity it is called the Paschal Mystery, the passover from death to life, from involution to infinite possibility.

In the present state of human possibilities, many of the technocratic solutions that we are hearing about carry the seeds of their future irrelevancy. This is the consequence of unbroken and unbreakable personalities trying to solve problems that are too big to begin with. The solutions that will be lasting are much more modest, personal, small, and tender.

Perhaps the economic system has to bear much of the blame for this distorted situation. We all have to earn a living, and that single fact, with all it implies, creates an excuse for avoiding the creative tension between the drive to mature spiritually (at the expense of the apparent or "false" self) and the drive to succeed and win approval. The intellecual, the altruist, the servant are written off by a system that does not even value the quality of its products over the measure of its profits. (Why, then, are we continually amazed to discover that capitalism hurts people?)

Under what conditions can humans evolve away from self-destructive illusions and toward constructive possibilities? How can we create "nurseries" for the "little ones" to become sages? We have to look for and nurture those local mutations in consciousness that seem to have both the global vision and the local modesty and sanity that make solidity (but not rigidity) possible. The scale we are calling for is distinctively human, even small. Yet these local mutations are precisely where the passion is; where the action and where the grace may be to create the conditions where Love, the energy source of the noosphere, helps along the vital discovery of oneself in the heart of others. In the course of creating environment and common work, there are rich opportunities for moments of growth—often painful moments requiring honesty, humility, and reintegration. Yet it cannot be sufficiently emphasized that love, confrontation, and examination of conscience do not actually make a community. Nor can we expect all values to be held in common. There is a middle ground between the vacuous conformity of a cult and the polite noncommunication of an academic department. The hope of this essay is that intelligent people can become truly wise, living and laboring with others.

There must be work: ideally, a balance of manual work and intellectual work that leaves opportunities for growth, difficulties, and recognition. It is sheer folly and pride to pretend that we are suddenly in a state of pure altruism simply because we have gestured our commitment to the life of a cell. The very reality of a cell is essentially something in process. But the process is *not* a matter of building community, nor is it necessary to be centered on relationships of varying intensity. Some work in the real world, accompanied by a certain affirmation and success, allows the possibility of relationships to develop in the way that such things happen—as a mystery unfolding at the heart of one's life, where actions are integrated into meaning and wholeness.

In the cells, in these societal mutations, the microcosm of the self may be grounded and disciplined in the ways of self-transcendence. Through this discipline, those who would be instruments of social transformation can familiarize themselves with the interior geography over which they will pass psychologically as they externally pursue a life of active political and intellectual commitment. The inner peace, of which so many have spoken but which so few know, arises from the conspiracy of love that animates the cell or sacred circle of persons devoted to personal integrity and global healing. Not from idealism alone, but from the doubt-ridden path of love and the ambiguous journey of faith and the imageless vision of hope do we find peace. This peace is not the child of technocrats. And it does not arise from the obsessive quest for personal peace and personal perfection "first." The time is too precious for us to bracket all that goes on around us until we have attained the status of sages. This time, the sages will be made by the very act of building the earth.

For the sake of "the little ones," I will be looking for the following things over the next few years—some modest proposals that, as they are implemented, will twist and turn us, bend and bite us with contradictions and inconveniences. And yet, all shall be well, and all manner of things shall be well.

1. Financial support for local cells, mutations, and alternatives directed toward a variety of visions of social transformation. Keep in mind that the evolutionary principle requires that the survival of a species depends on the emergence of vigorous variant forms that will be able to adapt to a wide range of changed environmental conditions.

2. Continued valuing and protection of the guarantees of free speech, free association, freedom of religion, open debate, minority rights, and popular election of governments.

3. A shift in diet away from processed foods toward the use of whole grains, fresh vegetables, and locally grown produce. A gradual decline of large agribusiness food production. A decline in production of meats and redistribution of grains presently used as feed for livestock for use by humans, especially in famine areas.

4. New approaches to health care including naturopathy, massage therapy, home remedies, neighborhood clinics, nutri-

tional guidance, and an emphasis on prevention of disease. Avoidance by more and more persons of surgery and drugs. An increase in the use of spiritual disciplines to foster and maintain mental health. A general cleanup of neighborhoods, waterways, and woodlands.

5. Revaluing the family and encouraging homemaking and child rearing as sacred and healing commitments. Widening the identity of the family and an end to discrimination against persons on the basis of affectional preference. The emergence of an ethics for alternative families from the actual experience of such persons. A voluntary decline in abortions.

6. Formation of coalitions of small local cells to achieve winnable issues with an eye to global consequences; a revival of the idea of "the common good."

7. A reduction in the number of governments, bureaucracies, and corporations to the minimum necessary to carry out life-affirming activities. An end to the shadow-government status enjoyed by multinational corporations.

8. A grass roots extension of these principles among Third World and Communist nations where they are presently lacking. A closer examination of the Chinese model of political and cultural development. Urgent application of sound ecological procedures and regulations around the world.

9. An end of nuclear weaponry; people will begin to demand this as they come to realize that these weapons are a symbol of a racial deathwish. Gradual end to the development of nuclear power in view of the genetic danger and the impossibility of disposing of waste. Vigorous development of solar, water, wind, and tidal power.

10. Cultivation of imaginative learning in schools which combine the two poles of traditional knowledge and culture with future-oriented creativity. Strong encouragement of language skills, literary studies, and general humanities from the early grades. High expectations on children, and high valuing of learning, and putting that which is learned to use. High valuing also of manual skills and crafts.

11. An end to naive attacks on religious and spiritual

worldviews by the intelligentsia. An end to belligerency on the part of religions or in the name of religion.

12. Fostering research in human transformation and spiritual evolution in the spirit of Teilhard de Chardin. This is to be given the priority that weapons development is given today.

Part Three

SPIRIT/SOCIETY

TOWARD AN EVOLUTIONARY THEOLOGY

Kenneth E. Boulding

Being neither a biologist nor a theologian, but an economist by trade, I bring to this subject only a lively curiosity, a deep concern about the matter, a sincere affection for the works of Pierre Teilhard de Chardin, and a mind uncluttered by too much reading. I do think of myself, however, as an evolutionary theorist, with particular interest in the application of evolutionary models to social systems, which is what I have tried to do in my *Ecodynamics*.[1] I am very deeply committed to the ethic and the method of science and I am also a participant in the Christian phylum both by cultural heritage and by conviction.

My father was a plumber. After a harsh childhood, he had a conversion experience as a young man, was a Methodist lay preacher, and a leading member in the Greek-columned Brunswick Chapel in downtown Liverpool, which we attended every Sunday. My mother and her sister and her parents, who lived with us when I was a boy, were all Methodists. In a real sense the Chapel was the center of our lives, a haven of quiet in the turbulent, noisy city in which we lived. With a scholarship to the Liverpool Collegiate School, where I specialized in chemistry, I became an adolescent skeptic. A Methodist summer school, when I was sixteen, convinced me, perhaps rather snobbishly, that people with first-rate minds could still be Christians. At seventeen I discovered the Society of Friends, which has been my spiritual home ever since. At eighteen I got a scholarship to Oxford and became an economist, and eventually an American.

These autobiographical details may seem irrelevant, but one's thought is a product of one's life experience as well as one's reading and observation, and cannot be wholly separated from it in matters of religion. With my mixed background of religious life experience on the one hand and scientific training and commitment on the other, it is not surprising that when I encountered the work of Teilhard de Chardin, especially his great work on *The Phenomenon of Man,* I felt an immediate rapport. I felt he also was a man who lived in a place between two worlds: the great, level and fruitful plains of science, constantly being mapped in ever increasing detail and ever widening circles, and the sharp mountain ranges of the spiritual life, with their heights of ecstacy and cliffs of despair, and a rarified air in which the breath falters. It is perhaps no accident that I came to live in Boulder, Colorado, where the mountains rise so dramatically from the plains, and where the biological species partake of both or of neither. There are species of spiders, I understand, on the Boulder mountainsides found nowhere else in the world!

To live with each foot in a different world may produce at times an awkward straddle, but it is never dull. One feels this in Teilhard de Chardin. He has one foot in the Jesuit world, where the Bible resounds like a mighty organ, with its great drama of creation, fall, redemption, sin and salvation, and an ultimate judgment. The other foot is in the world of paleontology, with its bible, not of words, but of the durable records of the past—fossils, bones, skulls, human artifacts.

We cannot escape the fact that science and religion historically have represented two very different modes of approaching the larger realities of the universe, and that the tension between them is quite real. Both of them come from what seems to be a universal urge in the human race to transcend what might be called the "folk knowledge" of our immediate experience and environment, and to look for larger images of the patterns of the universe beyond our own time and place, our neighborhood and our immediate surroundings. In the religious mode, the human race has tended to work from analogy. We see this even in the earliest forms of animistic religion. We are conscious of an internal unity of spirit—the "I"—within ourselves, which gives rise to our behavior. By analogy, we assume that there is a similar spirit within other human beings. This works very well. It is a short step from this to suppose that there must be similar spirits in the animals, the plants, the rocks, and even the winds and the waters. Such are the Kami of Japan, or the "light-winged dryads of the trees" of the Greeks. Just as we find that we can change the behavior of other human beings by speech and communication of many kinds, it is not unreasonable to suppose that we could change the behavior of the nonhuman world around us in similar ways, so we get rain dances, offerings and sacrifices, the Torii of Japan, the prayer wheels of Tibet, the libations of the Romans, the vast rich patterns of ritual that are expressed through all human history.

There is no doubt that such activities produce internal satisfactions and make people feel better in the face of uncertain and dangerous environments. Funeral patterns similarly follow processes of analogy. "But in that sleep of death what dreams may come," says Hamlet. We awake from sleep, why should we not wake from death? So come the great tombs, the sacrifices, pyramids, and the great panoply of the rituals of death. It may be indeed, as Julian Jaynes has suggested,[2] that in earlier times real genetic differences existed that made the right and left brains more independent, so that more people actually heard the voices of the gods. Somewhere about 1400 B.C., however, the gods began to fade and the rich imaginations that produced Olympus and its innumerable counterparts around the world somehow became less vivid and convincing. Monotheism, the Great Spirit of American Indians, the Lord of Israel, the Loving Father of Christianity, the all-pervasive power of Allah, the infinitely small point of infinitely bright light of Dante, even perhaps the "Force" of *Star Wars*, emerge as a formless but active creative principle commanding praise, devotion, worship, and prayer.

By contrast, science works not so much from analogy, although this plays some role in the development of theories, but by the formation of specific images of systems, tested as far as possible by observation. The observations may be by experiment in those disciplines where this is suitable because of the nature of their reality which is being investigated, or by continued and well-sampled observation through time, as for instance in the case of astronomy, to a considerable extent in biology, and in most of the social sciences.

I have argued that there are two epistemological processes at work in human beings. One might be called the "top down," by which we take the internal consciousness that we have of the extremely complex system that constitutes ourselves, and apply this to other systems, largely by analogy. This is the primary method of religion, but it also applies to poetry, literature, the novel, and a good deal of our knowledge of social systems and other people. The other is the "bottom up" method, which is much more characteristic of science, which builds from images of fairly simple systems toward the more complex. It deliberately reduces the complexity of reality by experiment, which is a sort of segregated simplicity. It seeks to simplify the images of complex structures through measurement, indices, and statistical operations. It works also with the careful observation of individual objects, crystals, rocks, fossils, the surviving debris of the past, and tries to build these into a pattern of how they may have been produced.

It is not surprising that these two different processes produce contrasting images of the universe. The human being is an enormous creator of artifacts, from the first eolith to flint arrowheads, bone implements, pottery, metallurgy, and space probes. We also look at the world around us and find it full of things that we have not made: animals, plants, rocks, stars. It is not surprising that we attribute these to a creator who also has made us, whom we have not made. "When I consider thy heavens, the work of thy fingers, the moon and the stars, which thou hast ordained; What is man, that thou art mindful of him? and the son of man, that thou visitest him?" [3] Creationism in some form is almost universal in religious thought and expression, and is by no means an unreasonable way to look at the universe.

The scientific image, because it is "bottom up," starts with mechanical systems, like celestial mechanics and Newtonian physics, which are not complex enough to create anything themselves, and the theory of which rather implies that they have been around forever, for they consist of patterns in space and time which can go just as well backward as forward. As science has developed, however, it has taken more and more complex systems into its fold, and as it ascends the scale of complexity there are some signs of convergence with the "top down" approach. We see this beginning perhaps in the mid-nineteenth century, with two very fundamental developments. The first was the rise of thermodynamics, especially the development of the entropy concept by Clausius in 1865, which introduces a "time's arrow" into the universe toward exhaustion of its original potential and toward ultimate disorder. The second was Charles Darwin and the beginnings of evolutionary theory, which suggests that there is another "time's arrow" leading to the development of complexity and the segregation of entropy, as Schrödinger puts it. [4] The evolutionary process creates islands of increasing order in the development first of all of life, with increasingly complex forms leading eventually to the human race and to its enormous production of increasingly complex artifacts.

In the twentieth century, with the development of quantum theory, the Heisenberg principle, and information theory, science has moved a long way from the simple mechanical determinism of celestial mechanics. According to a famous story, the origins of which I have never been able to track down, Napoleon is supposed to have asked Laplace, on being presented with his famous equations of the solar system, whether he found God in his system. And to this Laplace replied, "I have no need of that hypothesis." In this case he was certainly right. The solar system is virtually an equilibrium system in space-time. Its evolution had practically ceased, until the human race started it up a bit with artificial satellites, and there is no room in such a system for creation, no matter how it may have originated.

Thermodynamics by contrast implies a curious kind of deism. There must have been some original creation of thermodynamics potential, presumably in the "big bang," which has been running down ever since. Whether there is recreation of thermodynamic potential somewhere in the universe we cannot really say. Presumably, if it was created once it could happen again, which of course is implied in Teilhard de Chardin's extraordinary vision of Alpha and Omega, the universe proceeding through evolution to a recreation of its original potential.

As we look at biological systems, the "bottom up" approach begins to discover things that look like the creation of potential. Thus, when an egg is fertilized it has this extraordinary genetic potential in the shape of information and something I call "know how," which enables it to organize the creation of the organism. This potential, of course, is gradually exhausted as the organism develops and ages and finally dies, but it is constantly recreated as new eggs are fertilized. Then, in the larger evolutionary process we get a clear "time's arrow" toward three things. The first is toward increasing complexity. There is no doubt that we are more complex than the amoeba and that our brain is more complex than the chimpanzee's. Secondly, there is also a movement toward control, that is, the development of cybernetic systems, which isolate organisms from changes in the environment, particularly, of course, unfavorable ones. The development of the senses and of thermal regulation (warm-bloodedness) are good examples of these developments. Finally, there is the development of consciousness, that is, images within the organism that have some kind of one-to-one mapping of the world outside it and its environment. This goes through simple awareness into the self-consciousness of the human race, which enables it to develop enormously complex images of the universe around it, in time, space, and relationships.

The creation of evolutionary potential, or at least its emergence, is again a very important phenomenon. The development of carbon, for instance, created a potential for all organic compounds. DNA created the potential for all forms of life. In biological evolution there have been many "inventions" like sex, the vertebrate skeleton, the higher nervous system, and so on, culminating in the human race with "Adam and Eve," whatever their names were, who had the full genetic component of *Homo sapiens* and set off this extraordinary process of what I have called "noogenetic" evolution, that is, the development of learned structures which are transmitted from one generation to the next by a learning process. We are still a long way from the great poetic simplicities of creationism, but there is no doubt that science is closer to it than it used to be.

Nevertheless, the gap remains. It is hard to interpret the richness and variety of religious experience of humankind within the framework even of twentieth-century science. The enormous varieties of the mystical experience, the "practice of the presence of God," the rich technology of private prayer and meditation, the psychic satisfactions of liturgy from the Quaker Meeting to High Mass, to the overwhelming rituals of Greek Orthodoxy, the exquisite simplicities of Shinto, the intricacies of Shingon or Tibetan Buddhism; all this is part of the experience of the human race that can neither be denied nor explained by science. In order to practice religion, however, there has to be a certain suspension of the purely scientific world view in favor of a poetic image of a "living God" to which the heart and mind can go out in love and worship, out of which exercises come a deep sense of spiritual closure and response.

I can illustrate this tension perhaps, by a personal experience. Two or three years ago I happened to be participating in a Sunday service in a college chapel in which the hymn of Isaac Watts, "I Sing the Mighty Power of God," was sung as a processional. It was not too familiar to me, and, as is no doubt usual on such occasions, the words took on a quite peculiar significance, and I felt a strange empathy over the centuries for the rather odd man who had written them, undoubtedly, as a testimony to his own experience. The hymn goes as follows: [5]

I Sing the Mighty Power of God

I sing the mighty power of God
That made the mountains rise
That spread the flowing seas abroad
And built the lofty skies.
I sing the wisdom that ordained
The sun to rule the day;
The moon shines full at his command
And all the stars obey.

I sing the goodness of the Lord
That filled the earth with food;
He formed the creatures with his word
And then pronounced them good.
Lord how thy wonders are displayed,
Where e'er I turn my eyes;
If I survey the ground I tread
Or gaze upon the sky.

There's not a plant or flower below
But makes thy glories known;
And clouds arise and tempests blow
By order from thy throne.
And all that borrows life from Thee
Is ever in thy care,
And everywhere that man can be
Thou, God, art present there.

Isaac Watts, 1715

It is an extraordinary expression of simple faith in an omnipresent and almighty Creator, the loving Father—even in another culture, Allah, the merciful and compassionate. Over a span of more than 300 years, I felt a curious envy for the great simplicities of Isaac Watts. By way of reaction, I wrote a modern version in the light of the world view of science, which runs as follows: [6]

Revised

What though the mountains are pushed up
By plate-tectonic lift,
And oceans lie within the cup
Made by the landmass drift.
The skies are but earth's airy skin
Rotation makes the day;
Sun, moon, and planets are akin,
And Kepler's Laws obey.

Is it the goodness of the Lord
That fills the earth with food?
Selection has the final word
And what survives is good.
And nature's patterns are displayed
To my observant eye,
The small by microscopes arrayed
By telescopes the sky.

There's not a plant or flower below
But DNA has grown;
And clouds arise and tempests blow
By laws as yet unknown.
However fragile life may be
'Tis in the system's care,
And everywhere that man can be
The Universe is there.
Kenneth E. Boulding, 1975

I must say that I don't like it as well as I like Isaac Watts, but it does express, I think, the gap that we face.

Teilhard de Chardin, of course, was a Christian, captured by the extraordinary story that is recorded in the New Testament, the potential of which, like the fertilized egg, is continually being recreated in individuals who recapitulate in their own life something of the extraordinary social genetic potential that came into the world through Jesus and the community of the early church that followed him. This experience crystallized, after some 300 years, in the concept of the Trinity, that strange, abstract, and perhaps not even very poetic concept (not one incomprehensible, but three incomprehensibles as the Athanasian creed puts it so well). The general idea, indeed, is not all that unfamiliar. We could take an analogy from music. Music the Father is the potential in the structure of the human mind and the pattern of sound waves out of which music comes. Music the Son is the composer who realizes this potential in a composition. Music the Holy Ghost is the performer who plays, and on each occasion in some sense reinterprets the composition the composer has produced. This triune pattern is very common; we certainly see it in art, we see it even in science, in the real world which is the father of science, the researcher and discoverer who finds out about it, and the teacher who propagates it.

Unlike some Eastern religions, Christianity is not a philosophy produced by deep spiritual philosophers but a record of some extraordinary things that happened to some very ordinary people. Any comparison of the New Testament, for instance, with the Bhagavad-Gita will reveal this principle. The gospel indeed is "gossip" about some extraordinary events, written down some time afterward, perhaps a bit garbled but almost certainly not made up out of whole cloth by a philosopher or a novelist. It is like evidence in a court of law, in that the very inconsistencies of the different witnesses suggest that what actually happened may have been highly improbable and puzzling, but did happen! Trying to interpret these events many years later, the author of The Gospel of Saint John, wrote "the World was made flesh, and dwelt among us." This indeed is what the evidence of the existing records suggests, together with the evidence of its continual recapitulation in new lives. Everyone must judge the evidence for themselves but, certainly, Teilhard de Chardin never lost his initial vision of Christ.

It is not easy, however, to be an evolutionist and an orthodox Christian, and Teilhard de Chardin's own Jesuit Order clearly had grave doubts about the consistency of their extraordinary member's vast vision of the universe with their own Christian orthodoxy. There is something, indeed, in Teilhard de Chardin's vision that is almost more Hindu than Christian. Brahma is supposed to breathe the universe out and then in every ten billion years, from Alpha, the great act of creation of potential, to the final realization of this potential in the Judgments, in which it is recreated in Omega. It is tempting to rewrite the great introduction to the Gospel of Saint John—"In the beginning was the Potential, and the Potential was with God, and the Potential was God." Then one sees the continuing realization of this potential, in all life and in the human race, as the work of the Holy Spirit. There are doubts, however. There are many composers of music. Should there not be many sons who write the music for the fulfillment of our lives and of our potential? The claims of Christianity to uniqueness are indeed a scandal, which the Chinese find hard to accept, and over which Islam perhaps arose in iconoclastic protest. But those, like Teilhard de Chardin, who are captured by Christ, find it hard to look for another.

These are puzzling matters and may well in part come out of the tension between the right and the left brain. But this tension is an essential part of the potential of the human race. Religion without science leads into superstitions, the exploitation of people by plausible but false spiritual leaders and prophets, and into the horrors of the Spanish Inquisition and Khomeini's Iran. But science without religion could lead into unshakable tyranny and nuclear holocaust. Teilhard de Chardin did, I think, try to bring the ethic and insight of science and the religion of Christianity together. It can be argued, indeed, that science was a mutation out of a Christian society and that it could not have come out of any other for at least three reasons. The first is Christianity's profoundly working-class origins among carpenters, fishermen, and tentmakers. The second is its legitimation of manual labor—*laborare est orare*. The third is its belief in the spiritual validity of the material world, which is not *maya*, illusion, but an incarnation of divine reality. Science, as a continuing, developing subculture, did not develop in Greece, in China, in Islam, or in India, in spite of many early movements toward it in all these societies. Only in divided and disorganized Christian Europe did science reach the stage of cultural "take-off."

Teilhard de Chardin's attempt at synthesis will not be convincing to everyone. In some sense it was a failure, but like the failures of his Master, it is likely to haunt the imaginations of humankind for a long time to come.

Notes

1. Kenneth E. Boulding, *Ecodynamics: A New Theory of Social Evolution* (Beverly Hills, CA: Sage Publications, 1978).

2. Julian Jaynes, *The Origin of Consciousness in the Breakdown of the Bicameral Mind* (Boston: Houghton Mifflin, 1976).

3. Psalm 8:3–4.

4. Erwin Schrödinger, *What Is Life?* (Cambridge, England: Cambridge University Press, 1951).

5. Reprinted in: *Finite Resources and the Human Future,* Ian G. Barbour, ed. (Minneapolis: Augsburg Publishing House, 1976), p. 174.

6. Ibid., p. 175.

MY FIVE TEILHARDIAN ENLIGHTENMENTS

Robert Muller

As far back as I can remember, the natural inclinations of my being have always been to love life, nature, people—especially old people, because they know so much—temples to God, sunshine, the stars, and the moon. My schoolmates used to laugh at me when I repeated my most basic conviction, namely that life was "göttlich" or divine. Then, in my homeland of Alsace-Lorraine, I was taught that to be French or German was apparently more important than to be alive, for we were asked to give our life for one or the other country. I learned that my grandfather had changed his nationality five times without leaving his village. I saw pictures of my father once in a German uniform then in a French one. I was asked not to cross the Saar River, which I could see from my window. Then troops began to fill our region, fortifications were built, and twice our city was evacuated. The second time it meant war. Half of my family wore German uniforms, the other half French ones. I saw human horrors that were in utter contradiction to the beauty of nature, people, church, sunshine, the stars, the moon, and the cultures of Goethe and Racine.

After the war I decided to work for peace, and in 1948 I entered the United Nations. For the first years I worked there as an economist and I was privileged to be associated with some

of the great ventures of the international community, such as
the creation of the United Nations Development Program and
the first world conferences. These pressed me constantly ahead
toward a global view of our planet and its people. In 1970, the
year of the 25th anniversary of the UN, I was appointed director of the Secretary-General's Office. From then on I really had
to have a total view and I often heard myself being described as
a "Teilhardian." Father Emmanuel de Breuvery, a companion
of Teilhard de Chardin, had already exposed me to the ideas
and philosophy of Teilhard when I was working in the Natural
Resources Division of the United Nations.[1] With Secretary-
General U Thant, this exposure became ever more frequent,[2]
and after thirty-two years of service with the UN I can say
unequivocally that much of what I have observed in the world
bears out the all-encompassing, global, forward-looking view of
Teilhard. My own synthesis or ordering of all I had learned
over the years took place progressively, at special moments of
my life when I was challenged to explain what was going on in
the world as seen from the UN. I like to call these moments my
"Teilhardian enlightenments." They were all very pragmatic
and arose from grass-root observations of the world and its
people. As an economist, I had learned to observe, to analyze,
and to conclude. Nurtured by my love for life, for the world,
the people, the moon, and the stars, a rather simple philosophy
took form in me which has much in common with the vastly
more prestigious cosmology of Teilhard de Chardin.

From the Infinitely Large to the Infinitely Small

The first enlightenment took place in 1973 when I was asked to
speak to the American Association of Systems Analysts on the
subject: "Can the United Nations become a functional system
of world order?" I am not a systems analyst, but I tried on that
occasion to present the work of the UN and its thirty-two
specialized agencies and world programs in as systematic a way
as possible. I visualized the Earth as a ball hanging in the universe, twirling around its sun. I asked myself if there was world
cooperation in astrophysics, outerspace, and solar matters.
There was. I then viewed our planet as cut in half and I saw its

atmosphere, its crust, and its thin layer of life called "biosphere." Was there any world cooperation on these segments? Yes. Then, within the biosphere, I saw the seas and oceans, the polar caps, the continents, the mountains, the rivers, the lakes, the soils, the deserts, our flora, our fauna, and humanity. On each of these entities again there was intensive world cooperation. Then I saw the crust of the Earth, the depths of the oceans, the continental plates, our underground reservoirs of water, oil, minerals, and heat. Within the mass of 4 billion human beings I saw the races, sexes, religions, cultures, languages, nations, settlements, industries, farms, professions, corporations, institutions, and families, down to that marvelous entity called a human being. I saw the microbial world, the world of the genes, of the atom and its endless subdivision into particles and subparticles. And on each of these subjects, humanity was cooperating in one or in several world organizations.

I was amazed by the simplicity of the pattern which was emerging from the work of the United Nations. Everything was beginning to fall into place! A magnificent Copernican tapestry of our place in the universe was being woven by the UN. A practical network of people and institutions all around the world was working on Pascal's genial view of the universe, from the infinitely large to the infinitely small. There remained a few gaps in the picture but soon they would be filled too.[3]

At the end of my speech, Edgar Taschdjian, a Teilhardian biologist and systems analyst, told the audience that this framework was typically Teilhardian and that Teilhard had always viewed the UN as the progressive institutional embodiment of his philosophy. He also underlined the fact that the UN system today, both in scope and complexity, went far beyond any functional world system conceived by philosophers or systems analysts.

A Biological View of Humanity

During the same year, I was asked to speak at a meeting of the American Institute of Biological Sciences on "biological evolution and the United Nations." It was the time when the UN was embarking on the great conference on the seas and oceans. I remembered my discussions with Father de Breuvery on the astonishing, teeming biological resources of the seas and oceans. I decided therefore to present the UN's efforts, world conferences, and institutional arrangements in a number of major biological fields: the World Population Conference, the UN Conference on the Environment, the Law of the Sea Conference, the Habitat Conference, the Man and the Biosphere Programme, the World Atmospheric Programme, etc. and I found myself suddenly exclaiming:

> One could write a whole treatise about the birth of this collective brain and warning system of the human species. . . . All this forms part of a biological evolution. The human species continues to probe out, on an ever larger scale, the possibilities and limits of its terrestrial and perhaps tomorrow extraterrestrial habitat. This is one of the most thrilling and challenging periods of our planet's history. I am personally convinced that we will find the necessary adaptation of our brains, appetites, beliefs, feelings and behaviour to reach new equilibria and to select what is good for us instead of what is bad on our small spaceship Earth, circling in the universe, surrounded by its thin but so fantastically rich biosphere of only a few miles, containing all life of our solar system. . . .[4]

After the speech, Professor Ernst Mayr, a biologist from Harvard University, commented that he had never heard the work of the UN presented in that way and that he had felt he had witnessed a rare moment in evolution, namely the birth of a new species, a metamorphosis as momentous as the transformation of the protozoa into metazoa. Perhaps indeed the human species was entering a new period of evolution, a period of global existence, a fact that would be fully understood only by future generations.

Well, if a Teilhardian had been in the audience, he would have stated most emphatically that my presentation was one long, practical illustration of Teilhard's philosophy of global

evolution, of the noosphere, of metamorphosis, and of the
birth of a collective brain to the human species! What was happening in the world and in the UN was just one vast confirma-
tion of Teilhard's vision. We did not have to wait for future
generations to understand that we had entered the global age.

From the Infinite Past to the Infinite Future
For a couple of years I lived on these two "enlightenments" to
present the work of the UN in my speeches and writings, and
to make further international progress in filling the gaps in the
two Copernican and biological schemes. It was not until 1975
that I made a new "find." I had been asked to speak at a joint
Conference of the Audubon Society and the Sierra Club on the
subject "Interdependence: societies' interaction with ecosys-
tems." I tried to do my best to show in a sweeping statement the
main stages of our planet's evolution since its birth, our present
position in time, and the recently emerging concerns about the
future.[5] Again, it was simply a schematic presentation of humanity's efforts and preoccupations as mirrored in the UN: the
world agencies were increasingly called upon to deal with the
past (preservation of the environment, of genetic resources, of
the natural and cultural heritage), with the present (world conferences or international years on resources, water, desertifica-
tion, science and technology, outerspace, children, youth,
women, the elderly, races, the handicapped, etc.) and with the
future (development decades, climatic changes, Food—2000,
Education—2000, Health—2000, etc.). The world had never
seen anything like it! But what was happening was in reality
very simple: the human species, as a result of its expanding
"intelligence" and discoveries, was suddenly forced to visualize
the entire time span of our planet, reaching from our most
distant astrophysical and paleontological past to the remaining
six to eight billion years of our future! As a matter of fact, each
layer of our Copernican reality has a time dimension, from our
planet's total life to the length of a human life down to the
infinitely brief life of an atomic subparticle. Moreover, everything we are doing today has a potentially lasting influence on
the future.

I saw suddenly our planet as a teeming ball of incredible interdependencies, complexities, intensities, relationships, exchanges, streams, flows and long-term changes, floating and evolving in the universe, carrying on its crust a species which had suddenly been able to dissect, unlock, and analyze most of that fantastic reality, and which was beginning to change it in the most far-reaching fashion. What was needed was no less than a total Earth-science in space and in time, a science of all interdependencies, a view of the Earth and of humans as one evolving entity, and a new art of planetary management of which the first rudiments were being born right under our eyes in the first world organizations.

That speech brought me one step closer to Teilhard's evolutionary views. Father Thomas Berry, President of the American Teilhard de Chardin Association, considered it to be an important speech which bore out Teilhard's view of the Earth as a "living cell" as well as his outcry for responsible Earth management. Teilhard had drawn his vision from his work as an archaeologist, paleontologist, and evolutionary scientist. I had drawn mine from my practical observations in humanity's first planetary institutions.

A Spiritual Dimension

Two years later, in 1977, a new broadening of my views took place. The religion taught me during my youth had largely given way to the rationalism, scientism, and intellectualism so prevalent in our time. I was not at all concerned with spirituality and religion in the United Nations. But as a close collaborator of U Thant, I could not fail to be deeply impressed by his view that of all human values, the spiritual ones were the highest. I became accustomed to his familiar fourfold presentation of all human values and concerns: physical, mental, moral, and spiritual. I also discovered that Dag Hammarskjöld, the rational Nordic economist, had ended up as a mystic. He too held at the end of his life that spirituality was the ultimate key to our earthly fate in time and in space.

About that time, the UN Meditation Group and the various religions accredited to the UN asked me to speak about the spirituality of our Secretaries-General and of the UN. As a result of U Thant's influence and the necessity to speak about the subject, I discovered one further, fundamental aspect of our journey in the universe: the spiritual dimension. During most of its existence the UN had dealt primarily with the immediate, physical needs of humanity, such as the avoidance of war and violence, hunger, health, hygiene, the eradication of major epidemics, survival at birth, prolongation of life, elevating standards of living, housing, employment, etc. Several specialized agencies complemented the efforts of the UN: the International Labour Organization, the Food and Agriculture Organization, the World Health Organization, etc. Another major priority was the development of the mind through education. The United Nations Educational, Scientific and Cultural Organization (UNESCO) had been created for this purpose. The UN itself was dealing with the great moral issues of our time: prevention of war and violence, the development of justice, the definition and protection of human rights, the adoption of codes of conduct for the powerful, especially nations and multinational businesses. I had already seen the UN's scope vastly expand into space (from astrophysics to the atom) and into time (the past and the future). Was the UN taking the path of all religions which dealt with total man in the total universe and total time? Was it not inevitable that the UN would sooner or later also acquire a spiritual dimension, once the other priorities of life (physical, mental, and moral) had been met (*primum vivere, deinde philosophari*)?

I suddenly understood U Thant's belief that the world would be a good place to live in only when its four billion people would understand that they were part of total Creation; that the goodness of humanity depended on their individual goodness and internal purity; that our lives were not closed at the beginning and the end but were part of an endless stream of time. Then I understood Hammarskjöld, who ultimately referred for enlightenment all human problems to a greater, outside judge—to God—who believed that "in our era, the road to holiness necessarily passes through the world of action." Then I understood the visit of Pope Paul VI to the

United Nations and his plea to the nations to repeat their tremendous scientific and material achievements in the fields of
the heart and the soul. The lawyer-economist I had been for so
many years joined their ranks, for I had not received from law
and economics the proper answers to the problems of life and
death and of our meaning in the universe. I have come to
believe firmly today that our future peace, justice, fulfillment,
happiness, and harmony on this planet will not depend on
world government but on divine or cosmic government, meaning that we must seek and apply the "natural," "evolutionary,"
"divine," "universal," or "cosmic" laws which must rule our
journey in the cosmos. Most of these laws can be found in the
great religions and prophesies, and they are being rediscov-
ered slowly but surely in the world organizations.

Any Teilhardian will recognize in this the spiritual transcendence which he announced so emphatically as the next step in
our evolution. He had arrived at this conclusion both from his
archaeological and theological studies. I had arrived at mine
through three decades of observation and endeavours in our
planet's first universal organizations.[6]

The Human Cosmos and Happiness

Accustomed now to deal with broad global problems in time
and in space, and increasingly drawn by my work to universal
and philosophical concepts, I needed to retain a firmer root on
Earth, a more immediate, concrete, tangible challenge. I found
it in a question which increasingly returned to my mind, "What
is in it for me? What does this all mean for the individual
human person?" Creation, the universe, remote stars, the
Earth, spirituality, and eternity are terribly big words com-
pared with my tiny self. As an antidote to cosmic dimensions
and vagueness, I began to concentrate on my own personal life,
dreams, experiences, past, family, as well as on circumstances
and persons who had played an important role or left a lasting
impression on me. I asked myself the question: "Suppose I will
die tomorrow? What are the lessons I would like to leave be-
hind, especially for my children and grandchildren?"

The answer was clear: I had to find out by recording the most sensitive highlights of my life, be it persons, events, personal conclusions, or important turning points. Since my heavy duties at the UN prevented me from writing a comprehensive, well-structured work with a beginning and an end, I decided to write down my lessons from life in the form of anecdotes and stories. There were about fifty of them. When they were finished, I discovered that there was one constant thread, theme, or search running through all of them: that of happiness. I had always sought the maximum fulfillment of my "divine" life! I had been on the constant lookout for circumstances, examples, and people who would help me perfect the art of living. I discovered that for me life had always been the highest value, a sacred gift. I had been given the incredible privilege of opening for a few years my eyes, ears, mind, heart, and soul to the stupendous Creation and the world around me. I had walked through the festival of life with the wondrous eyes of a child. I had lived and loved my life with every fiber of my heart, with true enthusiasm (by God possessed). And that realization gave me the clue to my place in the total scheme: the universe is made up of endless cosmoses, from the infinitely large to the infinitely small; I am one of these cosmoses, linked with everything in the heavens and on Earth, endowed with a unique and unrepeatable life in all eternity, were it only because the external circumstances and companions would never be the same. How did the world at the precise moment of time when my human cosmos was inserted in it look? How did I relate to it? How did I find fulfillment in it?

Obviously it was a highly imperfect world, in which two-thirds of humanity still lived in utter poverty while 500 billion dollars were being squandered each year on frightful armaments. It was a highly immoral world, a largely nonspiritual world, seemingly abandoned by God to an unknown fate in the universe. I had seen all its evils, injustices, contradictions, and follies during a World War and during my thirty-two years of world service. Could I despair? Should I give up? Was the universe an immense non-sense?

No, because I was human, that is, endowed with the highest privileges and perceptions of any living species on this planet; it was up to me to "focus" and to sharpen these admirable instruments called doing, seeing, hearing, thinking, feeling, dreaming, hoping, and loving; I could focus my attention and love from a flower or a child to the universe and God, from the infinite past to the infinite future; I could profit from the incredible expansion of our senses through science and technology: my hands had been extended with astonishing instruments and machines, my eyes with telescopes, television and microscopes, my ears with telephones and radio, my legs with automobiles, trains, boats, and planes, my brain with books and computers; I could seek, know, and feel in myself the entire universe and Godhead, for I was part of them and they were part of me; it could not be otherwise; and last but not least I was the master of my cosmos, it was up to me to guide it, to uplift it, to give it confidence and joy, to keep it in an endless wondrous, inquisitive, searching, loving, and hopeful mood. And when I would die, it would by far not yet be the end: my matter and life would become other matter and life; my thoughts, actions, and feelings would remain part of the total stock of thoughts, actions, and feelings of humanity; there was only a change of worlds; even after the explosion of our solar system into fathomless space, every atom of this planet will again become an atom or another star, as it has been and will be for all eternity. No, I would never understand it all, I would not even understand a small part of it, and yet, to be alive, to feel it, to know what I know, to be admitted to the banquet of life on our miraculous planet was indeed a fantastic privilege, a mysterious, stupendous phenomenon or gift of God in the vast unfathomable universe.

And I wondered why all my human brethren in the affluent world did not have the same elation about life, why they did not share my enthusiasm and gratitude, why they did not consider life as great, sacred, untouchable, and divine; why there was war, killing, hurting, and constant debasing of life; why there was so much injustice, pessimism, and lamenting; why they did not help their poor fellow humans in the Third World; why we did not all love up to the brim our beautiful planet, our skies, our waters, our mountains, our seas, our brethren the animals, our sisters the flowers, our vast human family with its teeming diversity and dreams, down to each individual miraculous, unique human being; why we did not like, observe, penetrate our self, shudder at its divine, mysterious greatness; feel God and the universe in ourselves and make shine to maximum intensity the star which each of us is in Creation. . . .

Well, even if humanity did not have its values straight and believed that wealth, power, arms, glory, a nation, a religion, a business, or an ideology were superior to life, I would carry the jewel of my own life preciously and unscathed through the noisy marketplace. Even if I was alone of the four billion people of this planet who believed in the superiority, sanctity, and divinity of life (and I was not alone: just ask any mother or any deeply religious person), I would proclaim and practice this truth fearlessly, joyously, and proudly to the very end, be it in prison or at the top of the United Nations.

And once more, as I arrived at these conclusions, the image of Teilhard de Chardin came back to me. This time it was not as a philosophical concept or vision, but the image of his person as described in a wonderful story by Jean Houston. As a young girl, Jean used to cross Central Park in New York on the way to school. She often met in the park an elderly gentleman, who was either sitting on a bench or walking around. She talked to him and they became friends. The gray-haired gentleman seemed constantly afloat in a strange, endless, joyous astonishment at life. He would hold a flower or an insect in his hand and infer from it the whole universe and story of Creation and evolution. As William Blake said:

> To see a world in a grain of sand
> and a heaven in a wild flower
> Hold infinity in the palm of your hand
> and eternity in an hour.

The old gentleman had introduced himself and was known to Jean Houston as Mr. Teller, but years later, when she studied philosophy and saw a picture of Teilhard de Chardin, she exclaimed: "But this is Mr. Teller, my friend, the old gentleman in the park!"

And it was the same Jean Houston who, when she read the manuscript of my fifty little stories, said: "They are Teilhardian. You must absolutely publish them. They will help many people." And as if to prove the existence of noosphere, she arranged for their publication.

At this juncture of my life, after a long, meandering search for truth, the picture I have obtained from the United Nations' global observation tower is now pretty clear. The table of contents of a new world encyclopedia is ready. The agenda for the next chapter of humanity's future is in sight. But this is when the real Teilhardian period begins: with this vast fundamental, well-ordered knowledge on hand we must now administer our planet well, learn the art of fulfilled living, practice justice, love, and tolerance, and celebrate the miracle of life through individual peace, happiness, joy, altruism, and harmony in the endless stream of changing worlds. We must now prepare for a Bimillennium of Celebration of Life, free of war, violence, hunger, and despair; a world in which every child can keep and nourish his love for life, nature, people, God, sunshine, the stars, the moon, and so many other wonderful things.

Notes

1. See "Father de Breuvery and Teilhard" in *Most of All, They Taught Me Happiness* (New York: Doubleday, 1978), pp. 113–17.

2. In his memoirs, U Thant cites Albert Schweitzer and Teilhard de Chardin as the two Western philosophers who had the most influence on him: *View from the U.N.: The Memoirs of U Thant* (New York: Doubleday, 1977), pp. 24–25.

3. The speech was published in the *Teilhard de Chardin Review,* vol. 13, no. 2 (London, Summer 1978), pp. 79–82. Copies can be obtained by writing to the author at the UN in New York.

4. This speech is reproduced in *Most of All, They Taught Me Happiness,* pp. 182–89

5. See *Earthcare: Global Protection of Natural Areas,* Edmond Schofield, ed. (Boulder, CO: Worldview Press, 1978), pp. 583–98.

6. See "A Moral and Spiritual Dimension" in *Most of All, They Taught Me Happiness,* pp. 190–95.

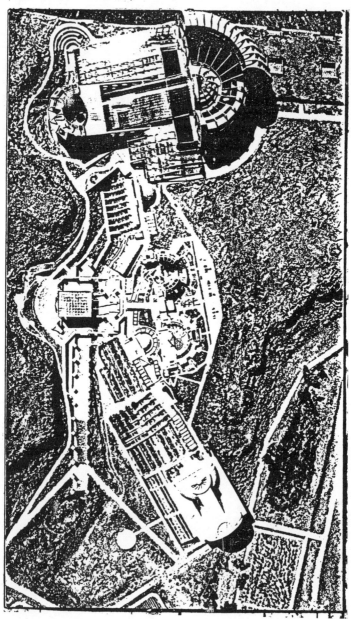

Aerial view of design model for Valletta Spring Structure, Arcosanti, Arizona. The design illustrates "Arcology" (architecture and ecology) on a mini scale. Developed for a population of 1500, the design is one phase of the 5000 population urban laboratory, Arcosanti.

MYRIAD SPECKS/TEASING GRACE

Paolo Soleri

I

These essays are to be "a sort of 'how to' manual of planetization." At least on one level the Arcosanti [1] project is already a contribution. Given an evolutionist's scenario, I see the enhancement of life and mind as inextricably bound to the urbanization of life and mind.

Urbanization is crucially dependent on the same logistical effectiveness that governs any sort of organism. This imperative is frugality of means so as to respond well to and to overcome the inertial mode lodged in "physical" reality. The summation of all frugalities, the well-known "do-more-with-less," is in the achievements of miniaturization.

Miniaturization is a clear, pervasive, constant characteristic of the living systems at the lower end of the evolutionary pyramid, and ever more so as one moves up in it. With miniaturization, life succeeds in developing the complexity of its occasions. The two, miniaturization and complexity, mount in tandem. At the upper ledge of this tide is the human organism.

The modality that well fits the complexity-miniaturization paradigm is the "urban mode." It can be said that life is an urbanization process, a process that sees things and events coming together in subtle and highly complex, miniaturized ways, and manifesting themselves as life—physiological, social, cultural, spiritual.

With urbanization powerfully present within all organisms and expressing itself with ever-better articulations within the species (see the interactive, cooperative, social nature of many of them), wo-man [2] went a step further and invented the city. Looking at the root causes of the Urban Effect and the 10,000 years or so of human urbanization, Arcosanti tries to radicalize the proposition by attempting to reinstate the working presence of complexity-miniaturization, quite probably in the best Teilhardian tradition. Therefore, the how-ness of Arcosanti is the quest of a more fitting instrument for the human animal to go on in the transcendental quest for grace—also a Teilhardian aim.

Perhaps it would be the wisest thing for me to stop here, but I will not. One can speak of hows when a kind of covenant is underwritten on the whats and the whys. Since I cannot sign the covenant as it stands now, I also have reservations on the hows of Teilhardian tradition.

To be abrupt, what if the admirable and engrossing edifice of Teilhard's work were to be deprived of its foundation: God? Could it withstand the storm of mind? I think that not only it can, but it would turn out to be a far less ambiguous structure.

So at the onset, I propose a God-deprived reality (that is, a different set of whats and whys) and then I wish to scout around for the appropriate hows.

I do not have the scholarly tools necessary to give full and persuasive arguments, but that does not discourage me from guessing and hypothesizing. My hunches are that the very reason why we are clumsy at defining the hows à-la-Teilhard is because our whats and whys in the Teilhard mode need revision. Revisionism speaks of disaffection, of ill-placed trust, even of treason. Be that as it may, my revisionism deals with a Teilhardian model that has been "robbed" of God.

II
What of God in a reality that has meaning?

(a) If God is not necessary, God is superfluous. (If life is not necessary, life is superfluous.)
(b) If God is predispositional (it predisposes), God is tyrannical.
(c) If God is experimental (it experiments), God is fallible.
(d) If God is creative (it creates), God is inadequate.
(e) If God is playful (plays games), God is cruel.
(f) If God and change (time) coexist, God is not the absolute.
(g) If God, the absolute, is, change (time) is not.
(h) If God is, then I, the discrete, am not.
(i) If I am (the discrete), then God is not (the absolute).

Even if one were to succeed in chipping away at most of those propositions, the remaining fragments would suffice for the dismissal of an all-knowing, all-loving, all-graceful reality. It would turn out that this reality, of which the hypothetical divinity is part, is a very wanting reality. The scenario seems to be then of a reality whose God or divinities are necessarily included in quest of an essential but elusive fullness. This sees Omega (the fulfilled aim) zipping away and for all practical purposes getting lost in a future too distant to be reasonably anticipated (prophesied). But then, eschatology does not deal with reasonableness or feasibility, but with desirability.

Since the absolute is by definition incorruptible, an eschatology that finds it necessary (desirable) to reestablish the absolute is more than self-confounding; it is self-contradictory. By the same token, if reality is not absolute (as Tao is supposed to be), divinity is absurd since one proposition excludes the other. As for the absoluteness of process, it would somehow seem the reverse presumption, because process is metamorphosis of that which is into that which is not (yet). If this were not so, process would be at best revelation: the unveiling (to consciousness) of that which is. But since the act of unveiling per se would be process, the whole thing is self-contradictory. The unveiling of the absolute disposed of the very concept of absolute. The absolute to which the unveiling is added (the evolutionary process, for instance) is defrocking the absolute of its nature.

The *mysterium tremendum* persists and the notion of divinity is inadequate. If divinity were real, it would be tremendously mysterious, that is, normatively ineffectual. If God turns out to be not absolute grace but clumsy or cruel, hedonistic or infantile or hopelessly tangled in his/her own hubris, we may have to be careful and deal with his/her demonic or imperfect nature on new footings.

I propose two distinct models of reality:

The revelational model proposes that the "best," if not the whole, of reality is there from the outset, is at the beginning, and that what follows is an uncovering, a revelation of such reality, an animistic reality in this case animated by the divine, creating, original act.

The creational model proposes an original condition of great deprivation, the absence of spirit and the progressive creation of it by the instrumentality afforded by the evolutionary process, a nonanimistic reality creating in itself the anima of the world, the gene-sis of Omega (seed).

I tend to believe that by inventing God, that is, by adopting the *revelational mode,* we can unload upon God all the deficiencies besetting the human species. Perhaps in a gigantic Freudian slip our invention of God is our way of saying that if even God manages to mismanage its kingdom, who are we to do better? This escapism is as good as the one that says that the infinite love of God will ultimately see to it that the poor, wretched, living kingdom will find redemption and felicity.

But what if the postulate, instead of being revelational, were *creational?* What if it were truer that an infant self-creating reality is beginning to see the possibility (dim, remote) of a process that co-involves each step of the process itself in the creation-construction of a graceful, beautiful, divine occasion? If it becomes plausible that evolution and God cannot coexist, but that instead evolution might be divinity in the making, it is up to our conscience to choose between the two and then begin to survey the equipment yards proposed by the chosen mode, to find which equipment is necessary, if not sufficient, for the task.

To believe and to propose that the hows applicable to the restoration of full grace, as purported by religion, can be the same as the hows necessary for the creation of a hypothetical remote grace is unwise and dangerously self-deceiving. I would not care to be part of such deception, not even in a year celebrating a great mind, in fact especially not on such an occasion.

Some points as to the two different eschatologies, revelational and creational.

Equipment Yards

Mode 1. *Revelational*

Given the postulate that reality IS and therefore that becoming is at most the unveiling (unfolding is the fashionable term) of it, it would seem that knowledge is all that is necessary. To improve knowledge entails the development of better instruments for knowledge. One improves oneself to become a better instrument for knowledge, a better mind and a better array of instruments, supportive of mind's work. Ignoring for the moment the absurdity of the co-presence of the absolute and of an incrementally better instrumentation for the acknowledgment of it, one could propose that, instrumentation being for real, life and consciousness would be, at different levels of efficiency or efficacy, instruments or means to the end of an ultimately acknowledged glory: God.

To be (and become) for the glory of God, a God that exists "in spite of" the means that are working at its acknowledgment.

Since the goal is supreme, any means to that end are good means. The process is such that if there is deception in the end, the means, good or bad, are coded (deception). This is not true if the end didn't exist yet, because then the means must immanently justify themselves. It is not easy to argue with a church that burns you at the stake if that is what is needed to save your soul forever; but to torture a person or to murder on the basis of a hypothesis, the remote possibility of Omega, is just not justifiable. The end cannot, does not, have authority necessary to justify the cruelty.

Here are some instances taken from the bins of goodness and necessarily within the revelational mode.

Benign Reality

Since reality is benign (created by a loving force) reality is sacred (a manifestation of God). Any action that alters or attempts to alter it is disruptive, destructive. That brands becoming with the indelible mark of an original, unredeemable sin. To become is to interfere in the grace of being. The rhetoric that becoming is moving into grace hides the fact that an action that intrudes into the absolute is an intruder in the absolute, period. White intrudes into black; black grays . . . To this perception of reality belong the outer fringe of the conservationist movement and the return-to-nature children.

God Created Humanity

Since the human phenomenon is God-created, there is an innate God-ness in *homo-primitivus* and his "natural" ways. Therefore, the tool-making of the early ages is O.K. The music changes when the abstractional power of mind brings about the technological revolution. Innocence lost, Prometheus on the loose; nemesis befalls the species via technocracy.

The idolatry of entropy (2nd law of thermodynamics) proposes the rationale of a life as elementary as possible, protozoan life for instance, because it forces entropic reality less to unwind itself.[3] Wo-man, the enormously complex, is consequently "the enemy."

The withdrawal-from-society people posturing themselves "humbly and appropriately" for the best possible revelation of Mother Earth (to themselves) are at the fringe of the appropriate technology proposing, sympathizing with the perception of an honorable stewardship of Mother Earth.

Small Is Not Better, It Is the Only Thing

Since there is a God-given scale to things, it is a sin of the first magnitude to develop instruments or occasions "out of scale" . . . a bad omen. But, 1) one wonders at the oppressive feeling a subatomic particle must suffer as it is subject to and co-author of events (organisms) that are trillions or quadrillions of times bigger than its puny self. And, 2) at the other end of the cosmic

scale one wonders at the discomfort of a being that is by definition as large as anyone is able even remotely to imagine (God is
all-comprehending).

To this perception (that small is beautiful) belong at the
fringe the zealots dedicated to the reduction(ism) of all things
which "bigness" confounds. The fact might well be that scale
and size are not at all congruous, compatible categories. That
goes also for miniaturization which expresses the gradient of
complexity and not size. (Is the elephant in bigger scale than
the mouse?)

Simplicity As Grace

Then there is the true and proper idolatry of simplicity. The
most direct way to respond to it might be to remind its advo-
cates that there seems to be only one channel that can afford
such a notion. The channel is the human cortex, that bewildering complexity playing itself out indefatigably, instant after
instant, within a few ounces of flesh. All the intuitions, inventions, prophecies, creations originating from wo-man depend
on this necessary, if not sufficient, complex equipment lodged
in the skull.

If what we call simplicity is anything at all, it is the utmost
complex synthesis co-authored by the cortex of the parameters
on hand. That is the very opposite of the (entropic) notion of a
pristine, innocent, simple, affective, wise reality. That is why
holy evolution is so generously but sternly working at producing ever-more-complex futures so as to transform the simple
nonliving reality into a complex, live, and vivifying process.

That the most complex of all hypotheses, God, may get tangled in the advocacy and production of simplicity points at the
absurdity of a model that proposes God and simplicity in one.
Only a frightened, envious, greedy but cunning God would go
for it.

Mode 2. Creational

The creational mode on the other hand, sees knowledge as the
premise for the "transformation" of extant reality into future
realities more and more radiant in consciousness and sensitivity

(complexifying). That is, *knowledge is not the uncoverer of grace; it is the instrumentation for the creation of it.* The difference is, at least in theory, immense. No less must different ultimately be the means, the hows engaged in pursuance of two such different ends: revelation of grace or creation of grace. For instance, time, the instrument for change, is for the first one the surveying device of the *extant* and unchanging landscape of reality. Time for the second is metamorphosis of the *extant* landscape into that which is not (yet).

If in reality the hows for the revelational and for the creational are not so actively different, it is because reality and life in it goes on creating itself no matter what the mind makes of it, and therefore the instrumentation willy-nilly is to follow suit. But how much more effective the hows would be if heart and mind were to be in the "right" place.

Running down the four examples relating to the revelational hypothesis, one can point at the contrast between the hows of revelation and the hows of creation.

Indifferent Reality

The understanding of an original reality that is not benevolent (revelation) but indifferent (evolution-creation) is only the first step toward a productive context whose task is to construct systems that more and more are capable of transforming "inert matter" into organisms or occasions radiant with spirit. Then the knowledge applied to good stewardship becomes the knowledge applied to metamorphosis with all the inseparable impending dangers.

There is another crucial reason for qualifying (if not disqualifying) a conservationism that swears on stewardship. It is that we all know that nothing here today will be here one million years from now, let alone one billion years hence. For a longer future even Mother Nature (earth) goes overboard. At the same time, a hypothesis that includes the possibility of a total recall, (implicit in the creational postulate) the total oneness of the end, would have precisely the effect of preserving for that special moment at the end of time every single bit of the evolutionary process. But for such a hypothesis the hows are trauma-prone (metamorphosis) instead of maintenance-oriented (stewardship).

Self-Creating Life

If wo-man is not innately good but innately enterprising (alive), his/her primitivism is not inherently ideal but just contextual. "Industry" is the way by which he/she tries to confirm and perpetuate his/her presence only inasmuch as that is the necessary premise in the use of the know-how directed at the transformation-metamorphosis of the context in which and of which he/she is. The apelike humanoid that began to "contemplate" the heavens was able to do so in the relative security and well-being of the family and the horde. His/her contemplations-induction-deduction activity eventually became that which made him/her humane. Industriousness, that is, environmental transformation, is the instrument, the technology, that opens the door to knowledge and metamorphosis.

For both Indifferent Reality and Self-Creating Life the food chain, operating in all the living world, is apropos to illustrate both the beautiful and bewildering miracle of evolving life and the deep, no less bewildering inequity of its modes. Naturally, it takes the delicate interplays among the synapses of wo-man's brain to propose sufferance as the pervasive aura of all-living and the inequity (a human category) that goes with it. Let's just say that fitness, that is to say, survival-preservation, means I'll eat you before you can eat me (I'll outlast you).

It then would appear that there is a profound and troubling continuum of inequity in whatever becomes (life) and that to transcend and solve the good-evil dialectic might take no less than a total and immensely traumatic transformation-consumption of the known cosmos into a pure radiant gene. This would be the cosmogene-sis of the universe the creation of an ultimate seed. Like any good seed, Omega seed *should* be "resurrectional." This proposition is the reverse of the revelational proposition that sees the "more" of the beginning, God creating the cosmos, getting tangled into the entropic unwinding.

Dimensional Congruence

The notion of scale as an icon to being human is understandable, but hardly meaningful unless the whole context is taken in. I propose that if the task is performed well (humanly), the system is right regardless of size. The ferry does better than the two-seater row boat or motorboat. The power loom does the same vis-à-vis the hand loom. The city organism better than an aggregation of houses, and so on.

Underlying the slogan "small is beautiful" are many not so beautiful worries. If we call the not small "IT," some of them would go as follows: Not being up to "IT," incapacity of being casual in the making of "IT," being afraid of "IT." "IT" is an intrusion in the status quo. "IT" is the unknown, the unproven, the incomprehensible. But if the hypothesis is creational and not revelational, the instrumentation has to be in scale to the wisdom, the compassion, and the anticipation of a process whose pedestal is maintenance but whose mode is transcendence.

Complexity as Grace

If reality is originating an aim out of its aimless beginning, and if such an aim has to place its hopes in a complexifying-miniaturizing process extending "forever" in the future, the instrumentality that "can do the job" must reflect and must be capable to deal with such progression. Therefore, simplicity is not only immanently dull but it is also eschatologically evil. It is an obstacle to transcendence.

It is entropy.[4]

III

What then differentiates the behavior of a society pursuing the revelational understanding of all that is, God, and a society partaking in the creation of that which might become God? Naturally societies do not work explicitly toward either aim because the components (us) are engaged in a mosaic of activities confusedly bunched and labeled: ego trips, altruism, social aims, political orientations, economic goals, national interests, caste safeguards, ethnic preservation, religious orthodoxy, etc.

The fact remains that the animal *in toto* expresses propensities and prophesies future landscapes, while the grinding of the components (us) goes on with more or less regard to minimal levels of decency, equity, compassion, reverence. Historical perspective helps to clarify the orientation of a society. Often in words, sometimes in facts, the revelational or the creational bias can be helped by the historical perspective.

For both revelational and creational hypotheses the professed aim is Godness, but given the different eschatological lights, the first one will tend to abide the Christian rules of altruism, piety, love, and equity; the second can only see those rules as necessary but not sufficient conditions for creation and for genesis for two reasons:

1) Equity and love pursued in revelational terms are illusory. The food chain, for one, stands in the way. Incantation hymns aside, the living reality has to face its own inescapable "violent" nature which is the very nature of organic reality. Wo-man carries into the human kingdom the same condition, embellished with the typically human additives: greed, fear, hypocrisy, ambition, cruelty. That is, the limited goal of revelationism is out of reach because of the very wanting nature of the "experimenter" (food chain).

2) Even if possible, a condition of equity achieved through stewardship and by abatement of greed, fear, hypocrisy, ambition, cruelty, would leave out the bulk of reality, it would leave out all of the past (debased therefore into means to an end), it would leave out the part of the cosmos not redeemed by the knowing of God. And it would leave out all of the future, separated from those ills only by the brittle, tenuous diaphragm of a moment, the present, of (pseudo) equity. Then it might appear as unavoidable that it is only by the demise of (cosmic) parochialism and the rejection of a dim-witted notion that sanctity is just around the corner (that is to say, that equity is achievable with the tools on hand, a benign reality and stewardship), that one can seek a leverage point making possible, if

remote, the chance for reality to become equitable and divine.

The revelational mode puts up (and rightly so) countless red lights warning of impending disaster. The creational mode better be damn serious in investigating the charges and act consistently with the findings, but it also has to be true to its own imperative: the creation of the, as yet, nonexistent: a nonexistent that is going to be unimaginably different from the present by the same logic that makes the present be unimaginably different from the past, ten billions of years of uninterrupted metamorphosis.

Then the "how-to" manual for a responsible present is to pick up the pieces of a still-alive composite of civilizations, reorder them, and in so doing transform them into more intense, more alive (more miniaturized), more interactive learning and performing enclaves. It is an active, willful commitment to the urban effect and what it means in evolutionary creational terms.

It is not a commitment to a religion, but instead a religious commitment. If religion means binding, it is like saying that there would be binding "religiousness" but without binders (religion). Binding would then be that which, in the face of harsh, indifferent premises (the "nonliving" and the necessary violence and inequity-prone process of evolution), encourages and confers staying power to the cooperative, interactive, social, cultural, reverential, frugal modes of communities. This would give them a chance to develop within a context, at least for now, of limited resources and energy, limited space, limited time, limited intellect, limited resourcefulness, limited altruism, limited imagination, limited knowledge, limited wisdom, limited compassion, limited love, limited grace. Repeating again that the limitations relative to all such categories compose a barrier to be eventually broken so as to reach, to create the unlimited, real beauty of Omega Seed.

If, on the other hand, all that is demanded is an intolerant or lukewarm endorsement of a religious dogma, or the dogma of stewardship, the search for and the application of the hows will not be much of anything. The malaise will not subside and the ego will eventually have the field for itself. Since there is nothing lukewarm about ego, its modes are then assured victory, the victory of intolerance and of self-deception.

Without passion in what we do, the future is gray at best. But if the ego is the passion, the future is full of dread, dread-full. To step out of the ego (Buddhism?) without leaving out the passion (Christianity?) is the "trick" that only a trust in something that transcends the values of the ego can perform. What I find unacceptable in the revelational mode is that since that which transcends the ego (divinity) has preceded and will outlast it, the ego finds great excuses, if not a lot of comfort, in ignoring the whole issue (rendered mute by revelation), and goes about its own not-so-merry way.

In addition, if I see the Almighty in God, my love for "IT" must survive a break through the massive barricades of suffering (eons long). IT may well ignore suffering; my puniness cannot, tempted also as I am by the hypothesis that IT might just be kidding around. (The hell with it if it were so.)

And if by chance I see in God a groping reality, I give to it a date and birthplace that coincide with the date and birthplace of the cosmos. Then all afflictions of the cosmos are God's afflictions, all wants of the cosmos are God's wants and defects and inequities. . . . That is, "God" is the cosmos. "God" is in the process of genesis, the genesis of Omega Seed (the creational hypothesis). If so, the Arcosanti project finds a fit within the evolutionary mosaic of hows because it endorses the creational hypothesis of an Omega Seed by way of a process-creation (evolution) working toward the infinite (grace-full) complexity of a reality metamorphosizing into spirit.

As a speck among myriads, Arcosanti wants to tease grace out of an immensely "unconcerned" reality, the mass-energy-time-space cosmos. This is a process that I think Teilhard de Chardin would find sympathetic.

Notes

1. Located in the high desert of central Arizona, 70 miles north of Phoenix, Arcosanti is an experiment in designing and constructing a functioning example of an alternative urban landscape, AR-

COLOGY: a fusion of architecture and ecology. The concept of Arcology addresses itself to energy resources in the environment and to the evolution of the human spirit. Today there is little doubt that our energy appetite must be curbed in order to construct the new towns needed to accommodate an expanding population. Arcology is a methodology that recognizes the necessity for radical reorganization of the sprawling urban landscape into dense, integrated, three-dimensional cities. A major tenet of Arcology is that the city is a necessary instrument for the evolution of the human spirit.

The completed Arcosanti for a population of 4,500–5,000 will occupy fourteen acres of an 860-acre land parcel, giving its residents access to both urban milieu and undisturbed landscape. The town will be integrated with a five-acre greenhouse sloping down along the south face of its mesa site. The greenhouse will provide food on a year-round basis and will passively meet the space- and water-heating needs of the town.

As Arcosanti completes its first ten years of construction, both the physical structures of the town and its community are in the first stages of development. Construction began there in 1971, and since that time 2,500 students and professionals have participated in the Arcosanti workshop program, building the town.

2. Wo-man (a small, affirmative act) stands for humanity.
3. The converse for complexity growing in time and thus unwinding reality at a faster pace.
4. Entropy mandates simplicity so as to postpone indefinitely the onset of entropic death. Unfortunately, this says that a nonliving reality is less entropic than a living one. It is also the death wish of a reality that having had a taste of life, says "no" to it.

Contributors

ELISE BOULDING is one of those names which comes immediately to mind in the context of world peace and alternatives for the future. Her work has included stints with the Center for Research on Conflict Resolution, the Institute of Behavioral Sciences (at the University of Colorado), the Women's International League for Peace and Freedom (of which she served as chair), the Institute for World Order, and presently chair of the Department of Sociology, Dartmouth College. Her writings have been as broad, including *From a Monastery Kitchen, Women in the Twentieth Century World, Children's Rights and the Wheel of Life,* and the *Handbook of International Data on Women.*

In the world or economics, men and women expressing a wholistic, personal and open point of view are rare. KENNETH BOULDING, Distinguished Professor Emeritus at the University of Colorado, is one of them. In addition to his urbane and powerful presence in the classroom and the lecture hall and his presidency of the American Association for the Advancement of Science, he has been active in peace-making and is sometimes called the "father of the peace movement." His published works include the now classic *The Twentieth Century, Ecodynamics,* and the recent *A Stable Peace.* He has been one of the supporters both of the Colorado Teilhard Center and the Teilhard Foundation from their very beginnings.

WILLIAM R. COULSON has long been associated with innovative education, the philosophy of science, especially the human sciences, and psychology. In the late 1960s he founded the Center for the Studies of the Person in La Jolla, California, where he continues to work among colleagues and friends, among whom has been person-centered therapist Carl Rogers.

Coulson is the co-author of *Man and the Sciences of Man: issues in the philosophy of human sciences.* He has also published *A Sense of Community* and *Groups, Gimmicks, and Instant Gurus.*

Few scientists have been as consistent and creative in presenting arguments and evidence for the continued growth of human consciousness as WILLIS W. HARMAN. As Senior Social Scientist for the Strategic Environment Center at SRI International, Menlo Park, California, he is at the heart of social planning for the future. As President of the Institute for Noetic Sciences, San Francisco, he takes seriously Teilhard's suggestion for serious study in the expansion of human consciousness. Harman is also the author of *An Incomplete Guide to the Future.*

ROBERT MULLER has been with the United Nations for thirty-two years. He is currently Secretary of the Economic and Social Council of the UN. He is also an essayist and author. His forthcoming book, *Global Spirituality* has been the subject of a thesis by Sister Margaret McGurn, "Global Spirituality: Planetary Consciousness in the thought of Teilhard de Chardin and Robert Muller," Fordham University 1980.

After studying Teilhard in France, where he collaborated with Jeanne Mortier, JEROME PERLINSKI became active in educational reform in the US, notably at Webster College. He has published articles on Teilhard, spirituality, and sexuality. He was one of the organizers of the Center for the Future and is now general secretary of the Teilhard Foundation.

ROBERT A. RUBINSTEIN is an Assistant to the Vice-President for Academic Resources and Institutional Planning at the University of Chicago, and Lecturer in the Department of Anthropology, Northwestern University. He has been a member of the Division of Research and Evaluation of the Atlanta Public Schools, and taught anthropology at Georgia State University in Atlanta. His publications have appeared in *American Anthropologist, Current Anthropology, American Ethnologist,* and *Human Relations* as well as other scholarly journals.

PAOLO SOLERI has through his theory of Arcology and the construction of Arcosanti, become one of the best-known architects of our time. Exhibitions of his work have appeared in nearly 100 public and private museums, colleges, and universities in America. Soleri was awarded a Doctorate of Architecture from the Torino Polytechnico, Italy; studied in the United States at the Frank Lloyd Wright Foundation, and has been awarded fellowships from the Guggenheim and Graham foundations. He has made presentations of his work and ideas throughout the United States, Europe, India, the Mid-East; he is author of four books, and is a Distinguished Visiting Lecturer in Architecture, Arizona State University.

SOL TAX is Professor of Anthropology, Emeritus, at the University of Chicago. After serving for three years as editor of the *American Anthropologist,* he founded and edited for fifteen years the world journal *Current Anthropology.* Dr. Tax is past president of the American Anthropological Association and of the International Union of Anthropological and Ethnological Sciences. As a Research Associate of the Wenner-Gren Foundation, and chief editor of the Wenner-Gren International Symposium of Anthropology, he worked personally with Teilhard. His work with "problems" of American Indians led him to develop the method and philosophy of "Action Anthropology." He has published numerous books and articles in scholarly journals, and has just completed serving as general editor of the ninety-one-volume series *World Anthropology*.

FRANCIS TISO began his study of the writings of Teilhard fourteen years ago. At the present time he teaches in the Department of Religion and Philosophy at Mercy College, Dobbs Ferry, N.Y., and serves as Project Director for the Center for Spiritual Studies, founded by Brother David Steindl-Rast, O.S.B.